I'VE NEVER BEEN THIS OLD BEFORE

STAN TOLER

HARVEST HOUSE PUBLISHERS
EUGENE, OREGON

Cover design by Left Coast Design

Front cover illustrated by Krieg Barrie

Interior design by Angie Renich, Wildwood Digital Publishing

I've Never Been This Old Before
Copyright © 2020 by Stan Toler
Published by Harvest House Publishers
Eugene, Oregon 97408
www.harvesthousepublishers.com

ISBN 978-0-7369-7956-6 (pbk)
ISBN 978-0-7369-7957-3 (eBook)

Library of Congress Cataloging-in-Publication Data

Names: Toler, Stan, author.
Title: I've never been this old before / Stan Toler.
Description: Eugene, Oregon : Harvest House Publishers, [2020]
Identifiers: LCCN 2019034731 (print) | LCCN 2019034732 (ebook) | ISBN 9780736979566 (trade paperback) | ISBN 9780736979573 (ebook)
Subjects: LCSH: Middle-aged persons--Religious life. | Aging--Religious aspects--Christianity. | Aging--Humor.
Classification: LCC BV4579.5 .T65 2020 (print) | LCC BV4579.5 (ebook) | DDC 248.8/50207--dc23
LC record available at https://lccn.loc.gov/2019034731
LC ebook record available at https://lccn.loc.gov/2019034732

Printed in the United States of America

19 20 21 22 23 24 25 26 27 / BP-AR / 10 9 8 7 6 5 4 3 2 1

I have chosen to dedicate this book to my newest grandchild, Bennett James Toler.

Today's research indicates that with the advances of medicine you may live to be 140 years old!

With that in mind, I will my positive out-look and my hope in God's future to you, my winsome and always smiling grandson!

Acknowledgments

Special thanks go to Jerry Brecheisen for his editorial skills, Adam Toler for his ongoing encouragement and support for this project, and Troy Johnson for his passion to get me published!

Contents

Introduction 7

1. Large, Extra Large, and Goodyear Blimp 11

2. Do You Have Something to Stop This Coffin? 23

3. My Funeral Is Prearranged, but My Death Is Pending 35

4. At My Age, Faith Takes a Lot of Works. 47

5. Looking at My Artifacts Through Cataracts 59

6. Imbalance Is Better Than No Balance at All 71

7. If You Can't Keep Up with the Joneses,
   Park Your Shopping Cart 83

8. It's Hard to Be Positive When You're Chasing Pigs 95

9. Is There a Topical Cream for Worry Warts? 107

10. Does This Bible Make Me Look Too Young? 121

Introduction

I had barely quit eating Cheerios out of a cereal box when I started eating preacher food off paper plates.

Preacher food? Yep. Church potluck dinner chicken—lard soaked, Southern fried, and crispier than a Kentucky colonel's upper lip—along with a paper bowl full of dumplings playing hide-and-seek in the drippings. Jenny Craig would have had a hissy fit just smelling the aroma.

I went from being a teen listener/ignorer in church to a teen preacher at 14 years of age without a learner's permit. Here I was, going through extreme puberty while trying to scare the devil out of grown-ups in pre-air-conditioned churches, where they fought heatstroke with cardboard fans that had funeral home ads on the back. Surely, somebody in the crowd was thinking, *Children should be seen and not heard.*

It was the dawn of a great life. But had I known I would be preaching this long, I might have spent a couple more years in the back row, playing tic-tac-toe on tithing envelopes.

Fact is, all three of the Toler brothers (Terry, Mark, and me) ended up as preachers. Brother Mark says we got so many spankings for talking in church, we figured we might as well get paid for it!

Wake Up, the Sun Is Setting!

That whole puberty thing was just a brief stopover on the way to the retirement condo. Time zooms! One day I was in the thick of an imaginary sword fight and riding a bike without holding on to the handlebars. The next day, I was waking up to a pimple breakout and couldn't seem to get a handle on anything.

Ah, puberty! My voice made a mockery of me in public, sounding like Frankie Valli singing "Big Girls Don't Cry" in a high tenor one minute, and Barry White singing "Just the Way You Are" in a deep baritone the next. I suddenly felt clumsier than a blindfolded giraffe on a skateboard. But that's the fun part. Other new experiences blossomed like tears on a *Dr. Phil* show. You know what I'm talking about. The dreaded first date with (fill in the blank) in your freshman high school class, and then falling in and out of "love" so often you get motion sickness.

And, of course, driver's ed! You brag that you "can drive already and don't need these silly lessons." Then when it's your turn, you get behind the wheel of that driver's ed car, put the manual transmission into first gear, fail to give it enough gas, and turn it into a bucking bronco. A classmate in the backseat taps the instructor on the shoulder and says, "I have to throw up." The rest rock back and forth, roll down all the windows for fresh air, and one asks you that heartwrenching question, "You sure you've drove a car like this before?"

Suddenly, grammar wasn't that important.

Onset of the Golden Years

That was puberty. It was a piece of cake compared to the dawn of the golden years. I don't know for sure when it hit me. Maybe it was the day I tried to read the warning label on my vitamin bottle and the letters looked like a blurry bunch of ants running a marathon. *Something's different here,* I pondered. But it didn't get better. The nears and fars got all mixed up. Soon I was thinking about ducttaping magazine articles to the far wall of the living room so I could go out on the deck and read them through the storm windows.

Then I realized it. I'd made the legendary leap from the pimple cream years to the Polident era!

It's a strange new world—a world of liniment, liver pills, and lumbar support. Once I only had to bend down to tie a shoelace. Now I had to rest up to make the trip (and breathe a liter of oxygen afterward). Things once taken for granted were finding the car keys, wallet, and the left shoe of my Rockport walkers. I think I could have lost a kettle of boiling water on the walk from the stove to the counter in an eight-by-ten-foot kitchen.

Vitality packed up and walked out without leaving a note. Once I had enough energy to propel a space mission to Mars. Now there were days when I didn't have enough strength to punch the volume button on a remote. Make it through the six o'clock news without napping? Nearly impossible! I vaguely remembered the headlines but missed the weather report. As for the sportscast, the last I remembered, Stan Musial is having a pretty good year.

Our Golden Age

I like the story of the senior man finally getting up enough courage to pop the marriage question to an equally senior lady. The setting was elegant. He had on his new khaki pants and an expensive combination dress shirt/fishing shirt from Bass Pro Shop. She wore a dress ordered from Amazon that resembled one worn by the Duchess of Cambridge.

The couple finished off their cheesecake. It was time!

"Sarah," Tony said as he struggled to get on one knee by the table, leaning on it with his hand as though the floor was giving way. "There's something I've wanted to ask you from the day we met."

Sarah nearly had the vapors. Her eyes lit up like the neon "WE'RE OPEN" sign at her favorite coffee shop.

Tony continued. "Will you be my wife?"

"Seriously?" the overjoyed bride-to-be exclaimed.

Just slightly annoyed and in pain, Tony responded, *"Of course I'm serious! I have two bad knees, and right now I'm kneeling on the worst one!"*

This is a book about the serious and the silly of living in the golden years with all their aches, pains, and victories. I dedicate it to you, my fellow travelers, in negotiating the cone zones of modern living. Don't worry if you fall asleep while you're reading it. I nearly fell asleep writing it. I've never been this old before! So, let's try to get through this together!

Stan Toler

1

Large, Extra Large, and Goodyear Blimp

I faced the dawn of my teen preaching years standing behind a wooden pulpit wearing a Sears and Roebuck mix-and-match suit and a scratchy, starched white shirt, with a pencil-thin black tie that looked as if a licorice stick was hanging from the collar. Puberty was all about what looked good on you. The golden years are all about what fits.

Once we hit 70, body issues are a big part of our lives. Some of our closest friends have put on a few pounds. Others have trifocals so thick they could read the stop signs on a road map.

Some pull fashion tricks, trying to hide curves with layering. At one family gathering, an unsigned note was passed along to a female relative that said, "I love you, but for the sake of our family's reputation, please don't wear capri pants." It had to be done. Another family member said the poor dear looked like a full-grown rhinoceros trying to cover its backside with a handkerchief.

Men have their own fashion strategies. Some choose dark-colored, tentlike shirts to cover six-pack abs that have turned to five-gallon drums. I guess old age is when our metabolism slows down to keep up with our appetite. The result is something we don't like to see in a mirror, and smudges of low self-esteem or guilt may keep us from getting a good view.

The Bible gives us a clearer picture. David wrote, "Come and see what God has done, his awesome deeds for mankind!" (Psalm 66:5).

God's creative work isn't flawed at any stage of life. His lifetime warranty will be honored to all that come to him for repairs. And that repair work starts in the mind and the heart.

It's What's Under the Hood That Counts

I've had some classic cars in my life. They weren't classics to begin with; they were just used cars in my price range. Why, I even had a Volkswagen Beetle—the German import that liked America so much it stayed. Mine must have had a temporary visa. It had a stick shift that wouldn't stick, a heater that only worked in the summer, and a parking brake that was so tricky I once had to shift into neutral and drive around the block to get the car stopped.

But the funny thing about owning a VW is that its owners felt protective of them. We bristled when somebody laughed about their shape and size or the fact that the engine was in the trunk. We just knew they got us where we needed to go without mortgaging our parents' house to buy fuel.

"You can't shake hands with a clenched fist."
—Indira Gandhi

Like cars, golden-agers come in different shapes and sizes too—sedan, SUV, and 18-wheeler sizes. Or, if we're shopping at Walmart for a new wardrobe, we might say we come in small, large, extra large, and Goodyear blimp. Most of us started out *S* and added *L* and *XL* with potluck suppers and senior discounts at those all-you-can-cram cafeterias.

Our shapes and sizes often define us. We look at the slim and trim generation around us and began to compare. And sometimes it seems as though it's comparing back!

My Uncle Edgar loved to tell the story of the preacher who finished an eloquent sermon on predestination at 12:01 p.m., much to the delight of the ladies' missionary society that had prepared the church picnic that followed. The picnic committee was kind enough to let the pastor and his wife go through the food line first. He had just picked up a barbecued chicken leg when suddenly the picnic chairman asked the preacher to say grace. Thinking he would add a little addendum to his morning message, the pastor said, "Like I was saying, I was predestined to eat this chicken leg. Now let us pray."

His sermon didn't go unchallenged. As he lowered his arm during the prayer (with the chicken leg still in his grip), a stray dog casually marched by and swiped it.

After the prayer, the embarrassed picnic chairman tried to explain. "I guess ol' Fido was predestined to eat chicken too!"

We weren't predestined to eat chicken or chocolate chip cookies or broccoli or anything else. We were predestined to make choices and to receive the approval of heaven through faith in the Lord Jesus Christ. What we eat or don't, and what our body mass or IQ is or isn't, does not reflect on who we are or what we can be in God's estimation.

It's what's under the hood that counts. Car bodies are useless without workable motors. Looks won't get a car to its destination; we'll only get there with a good motor. My VW had a unique shape, but it also had a trusty motor. As long as the engine was working, it didn't matter that there was rust on the fenders and cracks in the windshield.

David said it for us: "You created my inmost being; you knit me together in my mother's womb" (Psalm 139:13). Stamped so perfectly on you that it can't even be seen is an ID: "Body by God." Actually, God thinks we're in good shape no matter what shape we're in. We were God-formed. Under the hood is a God-planned, Christ-created, Spirit-affirmed motor. God is moving us toward his destination for us. Paul said, "I press toward the mark for the prize of the high calling of God in Christ Jesus" (Philippians 3:14 KJV).

It's the parts, not the paint job.

The Only Inspection That Counts

David's wonderful psalm continues with, "I praise you because I am fearfully and wonderfully made; your works are wonderful, I know that full well" (Psalm 139:14). David had a good opinion about himself—not narcissistic, but realistic. He knew the only opinion that matters is God's. That wasn't the case for one youth pastor.

The board chairman of a local church received an early morning call. "I'm calling about the youth pastor position that was posted online several weeks ago," the caller said. The chairman replied, "I'm sorry, but we've already filled that position." The youth pastor said, "Okay." And then he added, "By the way, how is he working out for you?" The chairman said, "He's doing fine. We're all satisfied with the way he's leading our youth."

"That's great!" the caller replied. "Do the parents seem to like him?" Puzzled by the question, the chairman said, "Yes, the parents seem to like him. By the way, to whom am I speaking?" The caller said, "Uh, I'm the new youth pastor. After that all-nighter last weekend and the broken stained-glass window and the water let out of the baptistery stuff, I just wanted to make sure I still have a job."

The moment we ask for (or are forcibly given) our first "seniors coffee" at a fast-food restaurant, we begin to be a brand. Manufacturers are keeping an eye on us, noting what we watch or listen to and sizing up what we wear. Why? Obviously, they want to sell us something.

My brother Terry is a well-known songwriter and singer. One of his favorite stories is of the time he was asked to sing at a wedding. The song requested was the popular song "If."

Terry said he did his best to memorize the song. But as we've all experienced, memory has begun to fail like a used engine with only one gasket working. The romantic lyric "If a picture paints a thousand words, then why I can't paint you?" came out, "If a face could launch a thousand ships, then why can't I launch you?"

Manufacturers want to launch us. They want us to be their living, walking, skipping brand. The only glitch is that sometimes we don't feel like walking or skipping. Somebody hit the up button on our age elevator, and the more floors we reach, the more down we sometimes feel.

Disconcerting? Of course. Now we're facing new challenges, like *ageism*. We're being overlooked for jobs as lifeguards! We're not being asked to model swimwear (unless the legs of the swimsuit are made of support hose)! We're the last to be chosen when the neighborhood kids pick sides for a game of dodgeball!

> **"The beginning of man's rebellion against God was, and is, the lack of a thankful heart."**
> —Francis Schaeffer

People behind the store counters call us "hon" or "sweetie," and they don't even know us.

God's Long-Range Plan

Sometimes, living in the golden years is as challenging as trying on our high school letter sweater. Who knew it would shrink so badly that our forearms would show? Like that sweater, the times don't seem to fit. Maybe our 401(k) shrank like that sweater. Maybe our "bonds" have us in "stocks." Maybe our insurance costs are rising so fast our blood pressure can't keep up with them.

"All the days ordained for me were written in your book before

7 Self-Improvements

1. *Improve your personal skills*—reading, using a computer, writing
2. *Improve your financial estate*—consulting a financial planner
3. *Improve your physical fitness*—exercising, eating better and smarter
4. *Improve your relationships*—spending quality time with family and friends
5. *Improve your networking base*—updating contact lists, making new contacts
6. *Improve your spiritual strength*—working on your devotional time
7. *Improve your leadership methods*—learning current leadership trends

one of them came to be" (Psalm 139:16). God wouldn't put us anywhere he couldn't keep us. Our times are in his master plan. We belong to him, so we belong where he is, period!

I was conducting a baptismal service in a Fayette County creek, and it turned out to be memorable for more than one reason. A six-foot-eight candidate stepped into the river. I looked over to my assistant, who, like me, was somewhat under six feet tall and whispered, "Step back a little." We moved into deeper water, waist deep, but the closer the candidate got to us, the taller he looked.

"Step back a little more," I said as the man continued to approach us. As we stepped back, we must have stepped into a drop-off. Suddenly, we were underwater, and the candidate was swimming back to shore.

To top it off, a smart-alecky parishioner standing on the creek bank shouted, "Hey, Preacher! Looks like that one got away!"

You'll never get away from God.

Open 24/7 Till You Get to Heaven

A husband and wife rushed through the front door of their dentist's office to the reception desk. "This is urgent!" the wife exclaimed. "Can Dr. Shmidlap do an immediate extraction?"

The receptionist hurried back to the treatment area and consulted with her boss. Returning to the front desk, she told the woman that the dentist would see her immediately.

Taking her husband with her, she met the dentist in the hallway. He said, "I understand we have a problem."

"Do we ever!" the wife replied. "We were right in the middle of our Christmas shopping, and suddenly there was this awful pain! There really isn't even time for novocaine. We have to finish our Christmas shopping! Just pull the tooth as quickly as you can."

The kindly dentist said, "No novocaine! Well, if you insist. Show me the tooth." The wife turned to her husband and said, "Honey, show Dr. Shmidlap your tooth."

Who needs that kind of care? It certainly isn't like the care David is talking about in Psalm 139:17: "How precious to me are your thoughts, God! How vast is the sum of them!" God is a 24/7 Care Provider who turns our aches and pains into gains. He has a grip on our coming and going. No matter how many times we listen to the voice that says, "You don't matter that much anymore," we matter to him.

> God is a 24/7 Care Provider who turns our aches and pains into gains.

Things around us are ever changing, and so are we. But what we are compared to or what we used to be is not as significant as what we will always be in God's eyes: "I praise you because I am fearfully and wonderfully made; your works are wonderful. I know that full well."

Cooling-Off Period

It was a hot summer night. The air con-
ditioner in the church was broken. Our
pastor was right in the middle of an
especially fiery sermon. Finally, when
he couldn't take it anymore, he stopped
his sermon midstream and said, "Would
someone open up a window and let
some of this hot air out of here?"

. . . .

2

Do You Have Something to Stop This Coffin?

Life in the golden years is mostly medicated:

- blood pressure pills
- vitamins and minerals
- allergy pills
- rubs and creams
- eye drops
- fiber supplements
- water pills

Every time we walk through the front door of the pharmacy, the pharmacist starts planning her next Caribbean cruise. We get one of those seven-day plastic pill containers with "S-M-T-W-T-F-S" embossed on the pop-up lids. Even then, the only way we remember if we've taken our daily doses is if we leave the lid up! (And most of the time we forget where we put the container.) Recreation is often another challenge. Golden-agers

> *"I told my psychiatrist that everyone hates me. He said I was being ridiculous—everyone hasn't met me yet."*
> —Rodney Dangerfield

don't realize that youthful flexibility has been replaced with the agility of the Washington Monument. Now if we win a tennis match, the only way we can get over the net to shake hands is with a step-ladder from Home Depot.

Some have a home gym, and after every New Year's parade, they start a fitness program, which lasts several days. In the meantime, their exercise routine includes a sit-up to get out of bed and watching reruns of past Olympics.

A friend of mine told me of being at a revival meeting where the evangelist made an unusual request. He said it was a Sunday morning, 15 minutes before the last parking space near the door of the local cafeteria was taken. The evangelist was waxing so eloquently that the pulpit was shining from the overspray.

> "God bless Mother and Daddy, my brother and sister and, O God, do take care of yourself, because if anything happens to you, we're all sunk."
>
> —Adlai E. Stevenson

He said just before the organist slipped to the Hammond, the preacher gave the invitation solemnly: "With every eye closed, and no one looking around, I'm going to ask you to stand on your head and bow your feet."

My friend added with a rather wry smile, "Hardly anyone in the crowd responded."

Even the fittest parishioners in that little church would have had a tough time standing on their head and bowing their feet. As a certified golden-ager, I can assure you I would have opted out. For one thing, I don't bend that well anymore, and second, it would be a health risk. (If I were to tip over, my injuries may not be covered by my insurance provider.)

Living in the golden years isn't a medical insurance picnic. As health risks go north, insurance coverage goes south, and in between, the insurance companies are singing "Happy Days Are Here Again."

I like the story of the elderly lady who sold fresh donuts from a cart outside a large bank in New York City. The president of the bank stopped by her cart every morning and gave her $1, but he never took a donut.

The kind gesture went on for several years. One day, when he stopped to give her the customary $1 gift, the donut lady said politely, "Sir, I really do appreciate your business, and you're one of my best customers. But rising costs have forced me to raise the price of donuts to a dollar ninety-nine."

Living on the Corner of Content and Discontent

The apostle Paul never wrestled with Medicare over a payment, but he did have some health issues that needed coverage. He wrote in 2 Corinthians 12:7, "In order to keep me from becoming conceited, I was given a thorn in my flesh, a messenger of Satan, to torment me."

I don't remember much about my birth, but I'm told that when my mother's doctor saw me, one of the first things he did was slap me! That was probably an indication that there would be a few worms in the apple of life. In fact, life is a journey from the *rights* of childhood to the *rigors* of adulthood. And on every birthday after 70, we are gifted with a new ache or pain.

Adam and Eve started it. The devil put a fruit bowl on the table, and they bought it like a buy-one-get-one-free salad at Wendy's. Unfortunately, they got a colossal case of "food poisoning" that was caught by every generation born after them. It was a poison of the soul, a "do-it-myself" attitude that resulted in their loss of perfect health. And every cut or bruise or ache or death since then goes back to their "menu choice" (see Genesis 3:17-19).

The "Adams Family" traded free health care coverage for a pay-as-you-go plan and moved from the Garden of Eden to the inner city, on the corner of Content and Discontent.

The bad thing is, they took us along in the move (see Romans 5:12). Because of their rebellion against the law of God, we inherited the results from the top of our headache to the bottom of our foot pain. And Paul's "thorn in the flesh" (whatever it was) was a lingering effect of the whole mess!

So don't blame the "Itis" brothers—Arthur or Burs—blame the devil!

On the Lookout for a Way Out

After a funeral in West Virginia, the funeral director assembled the pallbearers around the hearse for instructions in loading the coffin into the vehicle. The church was on a rather steep hill, and the hearse was parked out front.

Working the funeral alone and taking his eyes off the coffin for the pallbearer huddle, he didn't notice that the coffin lying on a wheeled carrier had started to move downhill, and it was quickly picking up speed. Soon it was too far out of reach, so the funeral director shouted to some pedestrians down the street, "Could someone stop that coffin!"

Of course, there isn't anything funny about death or dying, but ever since Adam and Eve, both have been facts of life. And people have been on the lookout for a way out, trying to stop their "coughs" and their "coffin" experience ever since.

Paul was no exception. He said in 2 Corinthians 12:8, "Three times I pleaded with the Lord to take it [his thorn] away from me." He had connections to the home office, so if anyone could stop the "coffin" effect, it would be Paul. But the truth is, he couldn't stop it, and neither can we.

I'm told the trip begins while we're still in our teens. Just think, you and I started toward old age (with all its pains, potions, and predicaments) about the same time we took that walk across the high school graduation platform.

And we have only limited resources to slow the process, like Noah's sons on the ark. Following the children's church sermon about the flood, the teacher tried to apply the lesson to the young worshippers. "Douglas," she quizzed, "do you think Noah's sons did any fishin' while they were on the ark?"

The little boy answered quickly, "Probably not much, ma'am. I saw on the Discovery Channel that the only bait they had was a couple grasshoppers."

Which Route: Fastest or Shortest?

We have GPS systems that take us from where we are to where we intend to go (as long as the satellite works). But sometimes the shortest route turns out not to be the fastest route. Another friend of mine said he was heading home, "listening to the GPS lady's voice boss him around a major city." Feeling a lit-

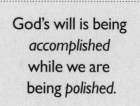

God's will is being *accomplished* while we are being *polished.*

tle courageous, he decided to disobey the voice and try a shortcut. He said the GPS lady's voice nearly had a nervous breakdown recalculating the route. And he nearly had one too when his shortcut almost took him through Mexico City to get to Atlanta.

Like Paul, sometimes we want the shortest way out of our health matters. We need to hear what Paul heard when he wanted out of the "thorn" issue: "He said to me, 'My grace is sufficient for you, for my power is made perfect in weakness'" (2 Corinthians 12:9). What's that? *Power is made perfect in weakness.* In other words, this

10 Ways You Can Turn Someone's Life Around

~~~~~~

1. Be friendly to a shy person.

2. Be an encourager to someone who lacks skill.

3. Be affirming to someone who has been left out.

4. Be a positive example to a negative person.

5. Be a mentor to someone who has potential but lacks opportunity.

6. Be a helper to someone who is physically challenged.

7. Be grateful to someone with a thankless job.

8. Be a cheerleader to someone who is discouraged.

9. Be a joiner to someone who is a loner.

10. Be a teacher to someone who is confused and searching.

pain has a hidden gain in it. Sometimes God takes us out of our circumstances, and sometimes he takes us on through. Either way, God's will is being *accomplished* while we are being *polished*.

Who Has You?

Speaking of GPS and routes, what happens if you only have an old-fashioned map and can't even read that right? While teaching her Sunday school class about the geography of Israel, one teacher pointed to a wall map of the Middle East and illustrated the distances. "See, it goes all the way from Dan to Beersheba."

One of her students, a young second grader, quickly raised her hand. With a puzzled look on her face, she asked, "Dan and Beersheba are places?"

The teacher nodded. The little girl said, "All this time I thought they were husband and wife. You know, like Sodom and Gomorrah!"

> Our enemy wants us to focus on the "what ails us" rather than focusing on the One "who never fails us."

Sometimes the route is all about the *who*, not the *what*. When my wife, Linda, was going through the tough times of colon cancer, we both faced the uncertainty of the route. But we both made the discovery that knowing *who was taking us through* was infinitely more powerful than *what we were going through*. The process was painful, but the outcome was gainful! Our lives and ministries were changed forever.

We thank God for his healing, but we also thank him for the suffering. Paul experienced that, as we see in 2 Corinthians 12:10: "I delight in weaknesses, in insults, in hardships, in persecutions, in difficulties. For when I am weak, then I am strong."

He saw weakness as an open door for God's strength. Our enemy wants us to focus on the "what ails us" rather than focusing on the One "who never fails us."

Our Lord may not stop the coffin experiences this side of heaven, but every mile of every downhill or back-up-the-hill is blessed, planned, and resourced before we even take the first step.

But He's Not Even Here

Trying to convince his Oregon church
congregation to take an active stand
against the worldliness of society, the
pastor began to list some of the problems. And then, with a heavy heart,
the preacher tried to drive home the
point. Taking a good deal of dramatic
license, he pleaded, "Oh, friends, if Jesus
only knew what was going on in our
society, he'd turn over in his grave!"

. . . .

3

My Funeral Is Prearranged, but My Death Is Pending

Those of us living in our golden years see things differently. When our eyes begin to become a little fuzzy, we go to a place like *Specs in Sixty Minutes* for an estimate. When we try to read the eye chart, "Dr. Onehour" places eye drops in our eyes that distort everything. That's to let us know what the world will look like if we don't buy glasses from him. Two hours and 66 minutes later, we make our way out of the store with a pair of industrial-strength bifocals and step higher than a drum major to climb over a curb to the parking lot.

That night we're checking our Facebook page on our laptop, nodding our head up and down, trying to focus. Then next week, it's back to "Dr. Onehour" for a reshoot. Probably some young thing at the counter will wait on us. She has the eyes of an eagle but tries to console us by telling us it will take a while to get used to the new glasses. In fact, it will be months before we'll be able to read anything without getting a stiff neck.

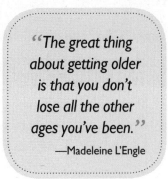

"*The great thing about getting older is that you don't lose all the other ages you've been.*"
—Madeleine L'Engle

Golden-agers look at life and death differently. Reading the newspaper, we hold it at various angles and lengths until the bifocals kick in. Then it dawns on us we have a new favorite section: the obituaries. Bypassing news, entertainment, sports, and money, we go directly to the obits.

We immediately look for the numbers—the birth and death dates. Any date near our own is a reminder of the mortality chart on our insurance policy. We envision the stockholders of our insurer, Barely Benefits of Boston, holding car washes to meet the payoff.

> "*Experience is that marvelous thing that enables you to recognize a mistake when you make it again.*"
> —F.P. Jones

Soon we'll wish we hadn't bought that $5,000 term insurance policy. Our beneficiaries will hardly be able to afford a balsa wood casket on a 36-month payment plan. They may have to settle for strapping us to the luggage rack (like the Griswold family's deceased aunt in *National Lampoon's Vacation*) for the trip to the cemetery.

There's More to Life Than Living

The preacher was having a serious talk with an elderly man who was known for being a worldly fellow but who attended church once every year. This year the preacher greeted him with, "Charlie, there's something I need to talk to you about."

Charlie said, "Go for it, Preacher. You know we're on close speakin' terms, and there ain't nothin' we can't talk about."

The preacher saw his opportunity. "Well, Charlie, you know you have quite a few miles on you, and we all have to die at some time or the other. I've been wondering if you have been thinking about the hereafter."

Charlie perked up and said, "Well, I'll be! Ya know, Preacher, lately I've been thinking about the hereafter just about every day."

Signs of Aging

Some used to think of themselves as a sturdy building of God, but then they began to notice some cracks in the foundation, some signs of aging...

- The plumbing and heating are on the fritz.

- The joints creak.

- The floors have settled.

- The glass in the windows fog.

- The only thing you can count on is the shingles.

"You have!" the preacher excitedly responded.

"Yep," Charlie said. "I do have a few miles on me, and they are beginning to show, especially when it comes to rememberin'. Why, I can be sittin' at the kitchen table and thinkin' about gettin' somethin' in the other room, and by the time I get there, I've forgotten why I made the trip. And all of a sudden I'm askin' myself, 'What am I here after?'"

The older we get, the more we think about the "whats" and "whens" and "hows" of our last days and the hereafter.

Jesus addressed the issue in the Sermon on the Mount. He knew we would have concerns about life and its comings and goings. So he advised us to put life in perspective: "Is not life more than food, and the body more than clothes?" (Matthew 6:25).

He knew how insecure we would be at key moments in our lives, so he reminded us that we were born with a *destiny* and the freedom to decide on a *destination*.

> We were born with a *destiny* and the freedom to decide on a *destination*.

He wants us to remember that our relationship with him is more important than anything else, and that he has our personal blueprint on the planning grid of heaven. He also wants us to focus on the "here for" as well as the "hereafter."

When the psalmist told us to number our days in Psalm 90:12, he wasn't just talking about counting the candles on our birthday cake; he was talking about making our days count. Jesus didn't promise us a living; he promised us a life—an abundant life, full of meaningful days. We ought to be thinking more about making our days count than counting our days. We ought to stay busy doing what we are gifted and called to do instead of wondering what's going to happen to us.

No Dis-Ease About Decease

We don't have to be at "dis-ease" about our decease. God wouldn't get us all dressed up in his righteousness if he didn't have a place for us to go! "If that is how God clothes the grass of the field, which is here today and tomorrow is thrown into the fire, will he not much more clothe you—you of little faith?" (Matthew 6:30). There are a lot of things we can be concerned about, but through faith in the Lord Jesus Christ, death isn't one of them.

Evangelist Sammy Sparks was preaching to my Ohio congregation. Known for the extended length of his sermons, the evangelist was advised before the service that the bus workers would have to leave the service at 11:30 a.m. to get to the buses even if the sermon wasn't finished. Seeing some of the workers leave, he remarked hurriedly, "Anyone connected to the bus ministry can leave now." He was taken aback when 375 "bus workers" suddenly took him up on his offer and made their exit. (We only had 12 buses running that day.)

Exasperated, Sparks then asked, "Now, is everyone through leaving?" An elderly gentleman seated in the middle of the sanctuary suddenly stood up, put on his coat, and started toward the aisle. "All right!" the surprised evangelist commented, "Let's all stand and sing, 'I'll be glad when you're gone, you rascal you!'"

Paul implied that he'd be glad when he was gone. He told the church at Philippi, "For to me, to live is Christ and to die is gain" (Philippians 1:21).

Life here may be tough. We may have eyesight, hearing, or memory problems, but, obviously, this life isn't all there is. God has an eyesight, hearing, and memory solution for us: heaven. "No eye has seen, no ear has heard, and no mind has imagined what God has prepared for those who love him" (1 Corinthians 2:9 NLT).

That's right. We have a prepaid reservation for an eternal, river view room in Gloryland, and our confirmation code is John 3:16. A place of new eyes and ears and no memories of past problems.

Taking It with You

"The pagans run after all these things, and your heavenly Father knows that you need them" (Matthew 6:32). Jesus gave the multitudes on the mountainside a pep talk on trusting heaven for earthly needs, and he warned us about seeking worldly remedies instead of God's provision.

Every once in a while some organization or institution digs up an Egyptian mummy and then posts pictures in the media. Have you noticed in some of the pics that the deceased have tried to take their treasures with them? Buried alongside somebody's mummy, there may be jewelry, tools, or coins, and sometimes even a dog's skeleton. The diggings prove the old saying, "You can't take it with you."

It seems as though many folks in the golden years spend a lot of time gathering stuff, as if they were packing their bags for a trip to the hereafter. How easy it is to get the wrong "stuff" perspective.

I heard of a news reporter who was given a campus tour at a local university. The university vice president serving as her guide pointed to a brand-new library building and said, "We haven't put the signage on this one yet, but it will be called the Nathaniel Hawthorne Library."

The reporter said, "Hawthorne? Do you mean it was named for the author of those beloved novels?"

"Not quite. It means it was named for the alumnus who wrote that beloved check!" But what we give or what we own will never be as important as who we are in Christ: children of the heavenly Father, recipients of his daily provision, and heirs to the riches of his heaven. God will never ask us to give something that he won't restock or replenish later on.

Pagans worry about stuff. Christ followers live by faith in God's supply chain.

God's Best Promises Are Out of This World

In the Sermon on the Mount, Christ gave his listeners a crash course in trusting his promises: "Do not worry about tomorrow, for tomorrow will worry about itself" (Matthew 6:34). You and I can't count on our tomorrows, but we don't have to worry about them either.

I heard of a new pastor who was trying to get acquainted with his parishioners at a potluck dinner. He had only been at the church for three weeks and was having a little difficulty putting names with faces.

Recognizing an elderly gentleman at one of the tables, he went over and sat beside him. "I think we met before. How is your wife doing?" As soon as he blurted it out, he remembered she had passed a few months ago. Seeing a puzzled look on the man's face and trying not to miss a beat, he said, "Is she still in the same cemetery?"

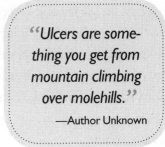

"Ulcers are something you get from mountain climbing over molehills."
—Author Unknown

Nowadays, that rookie preacher might be dragged before a church council and given a lecture on politically correct ministry! But it's not embarrassing to talk about death and dying. God wasn't silent about it in his Word, so neither should we be.

The fact is, death is a bonus for God's children. Dying here simply means transferring to an eternally satisfying life over there. Jesus said, "My Father's house has many rooms; if that were not so, would I have told you that I am going there to prepare a place for you? And if I go and prepare a place for you, I will come back and take you to be with me that you also may be where I am" (John 14:2-3).

I like the story of the couple who attended their high school's fiftieth class reunion. Most of the attendees were not only having trouble remembering the names of their classmates, but their heads were bobbing up and down like sparrows drinking from a pond in the front yard, trying to read name tags with their trifocals.

They were just about ready to play their version of *The Newlywed Game* when suddenly there was a hush, and their attention was drawn to the entrance door. A couple in their twenties had stepped inside the room. Thinking they had either come to the wrong event or it was classmates who'd had full-body plastic surgery, the class president wheeled his walker over to the couple and asked if he could help them.

Their answer set off several of the fiftieth reunion classmates' pacemakers. "No, thanks. We're the Medfords, and our high school class is having its tenth reunion down the hall. We just came by to see what we would look like in 40 more years."

Let's not worry about the coming and going of our years. God always saves the best for last. He not only has a place for us, but he has a crowd there who won't be worrying about anything!

Welcome, Visitors

Wanting to encourage his congregation to be sure to greet that day's visitors after the service, the well-meaning pastor asked all those who were new to the church to stand. Then, he told the congregation, "Take a good look at these people and keep an eye on them after the service."

4

At My Age, Faith Takes a Lot of Works

When I was preaching in Elizabethtown, Kentucky, my three points and a poem were going exceptionally well, and the crowd was expressing its approval with liberal doses of "Amen!"

One young man in the audience was a new convert, and his former biker lifestyle was quite obvious. He was a walking advertisement for Harley-Davidson, with a leather vest that covered most of a T-shirt (that covered most of a beer belly), and leather breeches that sat atop huge, scuffed biker boots with even bigger buckles on the side.

At least one of my points must have hit home. The newly redeemed biker didn't have the church lingo down, but he wanted to add his two cents. The heads of the "Amen-ers" snapped around like a bobblehead doll with a bad spring when the biker excitedly voiced his own brand of approval. "GO, BUBBA! YOU DA MAN!"

Golden-agers sometimes struggle with issues of faith—not so much getting or keeping it, but working it out in a brand-new "bubba" environment. The language and practices of our "old" church have been replaced with "new" church, and we're huffin' and puffin' to keep up.

Weekend Warriors

We face worship weekends with determination. We are weekend warriors, Christian soldiers valiantly standing guard over faith stuff that a new generation hasn't even heard about. They have a new way of expressing our mature faith.

I heard of a pastor who was using the unusually high attendance of an Easter week Sunday to give his fiery sermon on the judgment. Emphasizing his point with a fist to the podium, he said, "Everyone in this church is going to die!" Silence fell over the small auditorium. Then a youngster on the second row shouted out, "Not me, Preacher! This ain't my church. I'm just visitin' here with my cousin!"

> "It matters not whether you win or lose; what matters is whether I win or lose."
> —Darren Weinberg

Sometimes the church "ain't my church." It has a new paint job, and we're still getting used to the color scheme. For example, our eyesight has changed. We read God's Word faithfully, but now the print in our favorite Bible seems smaller than the eyelashes of a mosquito. And ending up with the wrong version can freeze our brains when the sermon notes on the church's overhead screen don't match our version.

Of course, we're still "glad when they said unto me, Let us go into the house of the LORD" (Psalm 122:1 KJV), but even the fellowship opportunities are a bit different. For some, the last all-church activity in their church was a gospel paintball war. That's a problem! First, we don't duck as fast as we used to. Second, we're not used to killing our brothers and sisters in the Lord, even if it's just a paint job. Third, most of our stretch-waist clothes are new, and we don't want to risk getting paint on them.

Serving is often a challenge as well. We golden-agers need our rest. When it's time to go to bed, some of us have to be dragged from a sound sleep in the recliner to the bedroom, where we have to remember our number on the Sleep Number bed. And once we get the right number (bingo!), we wage war with the Insomniacs (cousins of the Jebusites) until morning. So something like helping with the youth department all-nighter the next day is just about out of the question.

Oh yes, and for some, church music has left them with a blank stare on their faces and an ache in their heads. They began to think of praise and worship times as a boot camp, and the worship arts pastor as the drill sergeant. By the time they've memorized the newest song, Sergeant Pepper and his band will have pulled it to announce a new one—one that only they know, and they're keeping it a secret.

For golden-agers in the modern church, it's like picking up a dusty hymnal and having a twentysomething usher tap us on the shoulder, point to the hymnal, and whisper, "Put it down slowly...and nobody gets hurt." But it's not just the worship changes that put a cloud over our head. Some of us don't volunteer for the praise dancers team because we've been dealing with medical issues all week. We went to the minute clinic at a discount store and put our well-being in the hands of a physician's assistant who looked about the same age as our grandchild. She gave us a banker's box full of pill samples, charged us $85, and reminded us that we're not getting any younger.

So sitting in that church/former K-Mart store, where the former song leader's picture is on a "Have You Seen Me?" poster stapled to the bulletin board, is often as comfortable as riding a porcupine bareback.

"That Ain't Spurchel!"

Let's put all this through the filter of the Old Testament book of Habakkuk. The prophet was preaching to the Jewish nation about facing the Chaldeans, who were intent on throwing down their religious traditions and introducing a strange new religion—one that focused on idolatry. They were about to be attacked by an army of change.

Chapter 3 is the prophet's prayer for the kingdom. He starts by reminding them of the One who never changes: "Lord, I have heard of your fame; I stand in awe of your deeds, Lord. Repeat them in our day, in our time make them known" (verse 2).

Then he prophesies that Judea was about to have its whole world shaken. What would be the result? Barrenness (Habakkuk 3:17):

- The fig tree does not bud and there are no grapes on the vines.
- The olive crop fails and the fields produce no food.
- There are no sheep in the pen and no cattle in the stalls.

Habakkuk must have longed for the good ol' days of prosperity and peace instead of barrenness and turmoil. But he had to face things as they were and not as he hoped they would be or used to be. He had to adjust to the present so he could have peace in the future.

It's the same for us golden-agers. Working out our faith in the "new church" starts first in the mind. Of course, we live in a day of spiritual barrenness, when there seems to be a lack of "grapes on the vine" (fruit) and a lack of "sheep in the pen" (growth), but that doesn't mean new methods for sharing the gospel can't be used.

We might need to tweak our thinkers and remember that what was familiar to us in the beginning of our Christian life was radically new to the generation before us, and it wasn't accepted without a battle. There was a time when using a flannelgraph to teach a Bible lesson was considered worldly. And playing anything but the piano or organ during a worship service could get you five-to-life in the church nursery. Why, there was even a time when "Amazing

5 Things to Say When You're Caught Sleeping in Church

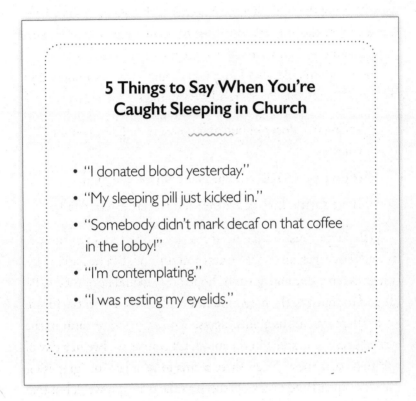

- "I donated blood yesterday."
- "My sleeping pill just kicked in."
- "Somebody didn't mark decaf on that coffee in the lobby!"
- "I'm contemplating."
- "I was resting my eyelids."

Grace" was considered too racy to be sung in church. And "Rock of Ages" was too contemporary for some. "That ain't *spurchel*!"

But the God who brings new mercies to our day, morning by morning, can use new methods (and yes, new music) that have been dedicated to him for the spreading of the old gospel and the discipleship of new saints.

Does Will Still Go to This Church?

I like the story of one family's contribution to the church supper. It was the Friday night before the church supper on Sunday. Mother had signed up to bring her famous lemon cake with white icing. Because Father always liked to raid the refrigerator during football games on TV, she decided to put the leftovers on a plate, cover it with aluminum foil, and put it on the top shelf in the fridge.

Sunday afternoon came, and sure enough, Father made his way to the refrigerator. "Honey! Where's that plate of leftovers you said was in here?" he hollered. "It's on the top shelf of the fridge, covered with tin foil!" Mother answered.

Father's next words brought cold chills to Mother. "No, it's not! The only thing covered in tin foil on the top shelf of the fridge is a plate of your lemon cake!" Mother could only imagine the look on the faces of the volunteers at the church supper when they uncovered what they thought was her lemon cake and discovered the carcass of a dead chicken, two slightly smashed deviled eggs, a smattering of broccoli and beans, and a cob of sweet corn with only one row of kernels left uneaten.

Habakkuk the prophet had to make some adjustments to keep his faith in working order. "Yet I will rejoice in the LORD, I will be joyful in God my Savior" (verse 18). He wasn't going to let the stuff of life get in the way of his worship. The obstacles weren't going to be bigger than the object: worship. That's a pretty good goal for us.

We might not like the order of service, but we didn't come to church to order the service. We came to worship the God who made order out of chaos, and who can turn a thunderstorm into a symphony.

The question is, "Does Will still go to this church?" The one thing that can't be missing in any church experience is the will to worship. We might come to church expecting lemon cake and have to settle for one row of kernels on the cob, but we can keep our eyes on the cross (even if its replica isn't on the platform anymore).

"Cracker, Please."

Habakkuk's prophesy also included a promise: "He enables me to tread on the heights" (verse 19). Whatever we want from God, he is willing and ready to give. God will always help us reach new heights. We might have to maneuver around some orange cones in the road to get there, but our determination combined with God's inspiration can make any church—or church experience—a temple.

It's like the brother and sister in a communion service at a Methodist church in Arkansas. The church had some pretty strict rules about participating in the communion service. No one under five years of age was allowed to go up to the altar.

The pastor gave the solemn invitation. Brother started out, and then he turned to his four-year-old sister and said, "C'mon. Aren't you going up there?" Upset, the little girl reminded her brother out loud, "No! The preacher says I'm too little!" And then she quietly added, "But could you bring me back a cracker?" If all we can get is a spiritual cracker out of a worship experience, then let's eat it to our heart's content!

Faith works even if you have to work at it. David said, "The righteous will flourish like a palm tree, they will grow like a cedar of Lebanon; planted in the house of the LORD, they will flourish in the courts of our God. They will still bear fruit in old age, they will stay fresh and green" (Psalm 92:12-14).

> The end of our beginnings doesn't necessarily mean the beginning of the end.

Whether we're within reach of Social Security or just a few blocks away from assisted living, God will give us enough of his "flourish" to please him, to grow in our faith, and to serve others. Maybe there will be a time later on when we'll have to be tied up to a support stake like a tomato vine. But like that ol' vine, we'll still be bearing fruit if we keep our heart aligned with the Gardener.

The end of our beginnings doesn't necessarily mean the beginning of the end. Hair, teeth, nails, and brain cells may not be producing much new anymore, but God promises us a "fresh and green" heart.

Where Are You Calling from Again?

Mr. Johnson, a businessman from Wisconsin, went on a business trip to Louisiana. He immediately sent an email back to his wife, Jean. Unfortunately, he mistyped a letter, and the email ended up going to a Mrs. Joan Johnson, the wife of a preacher who just passed away.

The preacher's wife took one look at the email and promptly fainted. When she was revived, she nervously pointed to the message, which read: "Arrived safely, but it sure is hot down here!"

. . . .

5

Looking at My Artifacts Through Cataracts

Solomon was a wise guy. No, really! Solomon was a Wise guy (maybe with a giant *W* on his tunic). How wise? The Bible says, "God gave Solomon wisdom and very great insight, and a breadth of understanding as measureless as the sand on the seashore" (1 Kings 4:29). He was wise enough to take a mental video of life and turn it into a travelogue. But I think he had a sinus headache when he gave the summary: "'Meaningless! Meaningless!' says the Teacher. 'Utterly meaningless! Everything is meaningless'" (Ecclesiastes 1:2).

At that moment, his attitude wasn't a lot different than those golden-agers who have their own questions about life and fitting in. Let me illustrate. If you're looking for meaning and purpose in your life, you won't find it on garbage day. Just getting the trash to the curb is an exercise in "utterly meaningless."

First, you have to get the plastic garbage bag open. No matter how well you plan or how determined you are, once you get the bag rolled out of the box and try to open it, the opening for the bag will *always* be on the opposite end and sealed together tighter than a reusable package of deli turkey.

Then, because you forgot to take out the trash last week, you have to fit into bags two weeks' worth of used coffee grounds, left-over pizza crusts, blackened banana peels, nonfat milk cartons, bread heels with bluish corners, a lifetime-guaranteed coffeemaker, and that ugly sweater you hid and your spouse found. They will share space with those molded plastic containers manufactured in an unfriendly neighboring country to humiliate us (and can't be opened without borrowing the Jaws of Life from the local fire department).

> "My opinions may have changed, but not the fact that I am right."
> —Ashleigh Brilliant

And, sure enough, the minute you step out of the door wearing the *Star Wars* bathrobe your grandkids got you for Christmas, carrying the bag(s) that are now leaking orange juice all the way down the driveway, the uppity president of the neighborhood association will drive by.

It's a good thing that the *meaning* of life isn't derived from those *demeaning* moments. And speaking of meaning, golden-agers often lose theirs. Retirement, reassignment, or confinement can be times when we began to wonder where we fit in.

We ask questions of ourselves:

- "Why doesn't my opinion matter anymore?"
- "Do people really appreciate what I've done?"
- "Can God really use me in this condition?"

I saw a cartoon of a golden-ager "sitting large" on an examining table in his doctor's office. In the caption, the doctor tells him to stay in shape. The patient replies, "I do stay in shape. This is the shape I stay in!"

David settled the question in his own mind: "All the days ordained for me were written in your book before one of them came to be" (Psalm 139:16).

"All the days..." God loves us—fused or confused, trim or filled to the brim.

Taking the "Mean" Out of Meaning

In the Old Testament book of Ecclesiastes, Solomon gave us some extra-wise advice. For example, he said, "When times are good, be happy; but when times are bad, consider this: God has made the one as well as the other" (7:14).

I've had management moments when I wondered whether I should have stayed in the haircutting profession (my part-time job in college days). And I've had preaching times when my enthusiasm grabbed my common sense and made it sit still in a corner.

Take, for instance, that morning on the platform when I was trying to build an introduction to a sermon on the Ethiopian eunuch that would surely go viral on YouTube. The audience was with me until I overemphasized the point.

"This Ethiopian eunuch was a man of splendid character. He was a loyal servant, he was trusted by the queen, and he was even treasurer of the court." I should've left out my next line: "And, no doubt, the Ethiopian eunuch was a good husband and father to his family."

Yep, we're in the "wonder" years, wondering about a lot of things, including why we said some things, and where we will store all the stuff we've collected over the years. Golden-agers have artifacts that have multiplied like coat hangers and plastic shopping bags.

We try to memorialize our lives with picture albums, souvenirs, coffee mugs, antique furniture, or ball caps. Then we make the startling discovery that the next generation has no interest in anything that's more than 24 hours old! So some of our prized artifacts will be displayed on the shelves of the local Goodwill store, and others scattered like dead twigs across the lawn in a moving sale.

We begin to see our stuff through the eyes of Solomon: "All is meaningless." But it's not meaningless when we see things in context. Stuff is meaningless when we think it's more important than eternal things, if we give it priority over faith or family.

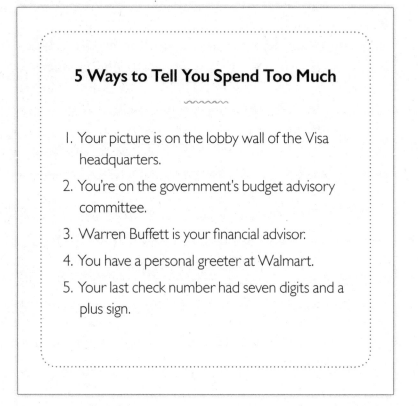

5 Ways to Tell You Spend Too Much

1. Your picture is on the lobby wall of the Visa headquarters.

2. You're on the government's budget advisory committee.

3. Warren Buffett is your financial advisor.

4. You have a personal greeter at Walmart.

5. Your last check number had seven digits and a plus sign.

Let's take the "mean" out of "meaning." The bottom line is that God has blessed us with everything we are and everything we have. "Every good and perfect gift is from above, coming down from the Father of the heavenly lights, who does not change" (James 1:17). *Who* we are is *changeless and good at any age*, especially if *who we are* has been given back to God through faith in Jesus Christ. And *what* we have is *good* as we acknowledge its source and honor God with our stewardship of stuff.

If You Go with the Flow, Eventually You'll Learn How to Swim

Solomon said, "No one can discover anything about their future" (Ecclesiastes 7:14). It was Thanksgiving Sunday, and the children's church director decided to have a question-and-answer session to teach the children about being thankful.

"How many of you are thankful for all God has given to you?" she asked. Hands flew into the air like scared pigeons. "And what one thing could we do to show God how thankful we are?" she quizzed. One little girl kept her hand up until she was noticed. "I know!"

"Yes, Shelly?"

Shelly replied excitedly, "I could give my brother back to him!"

If we try to build our future on the foundations of our past, we will always be frustrated.

Every once in a while, I catch myself getting stuck in rewind, thinking about the wonderful opportunities that have been mine during 50-plus years of ministry.

Over those years, I've flown to so many places and received so many frequent flyer points that I'm almost sure I'll be bumped up to first class in the rapture! But *who* I am is not *where* I've been or *what* I've done. *Who I am* is *what I am doing right now* to fulfill the calling God has placed on my life.

The apostle Paul spelled that out as clear as crystal: "One thing I do: Forgetting what is behind and straining toward what is ahead, I press on toward the goal to win the prize for which God has called me heavenward in Christ Jesus" (Philippians 3:13-14).

I'm in the flow of life, learning how to swim in the waters where God has placed me. I'm answering the call to be myself and to use what God has gifted me with to be a positive influence in my culture to my generation.

The History Channel Always Shows Repeats

The little town of Baileysville, West Virginia, where I grew up, didn't have a lot of TV viewing options. And for a long time, there weren't *any* television options in the Toler house. When we finally got one of those first TVs (the cabinet was the size of Yankee stadium and the screen was as tiny as a matchbox), the only way we got close to a channel was to wrap aluminum foil around our rabbit ears antennae and con my younger brother, Mark, into twisting and turning the ears until the fuzz cleared up enough to catch the last half of *Bonanza*. (Mark may have invented Chubby Checker's "Twist!")

Nowadays, there are more TV viewing options than there are politicians at a Fourth of July picnic in an election year. And isn't it funny that with all those channels and their hundreds of programs, we often settle on watching reruns of *I Love Lucy*? Why? The TV schedulers say those programs serve as a night-light, a constant and reassuring source of sameness.

I'll admit it. Sometimes sameness feels good. That's probably because once when I wasn't looking, life threw a knuckleball at me. One trip to the doctor's office can do that. No wonder Solomon wrote, "I have seen both of these: the righteous perishing in their righteousness, and the wicked living long in their wickedness"

(Ecclesiastes 7:15). In other words, life will always be just a bubble off. Each New Year may put some thorns in our Rose Parade.

Since I upgraded from that nine-inch TV, I like to watch the History Channel once in a while. (My boys say it's because I was there when the ancient events actually happened!) That channel proves that what goes around comes around, including some traumatic times. Job explained, "Man is born to trouble as surely as sparks fly upward" (Job 5:7).

Your story is on the History Channel of life along with the stories of countless others. And our meaning comes from understanding our place in the mess. God has brought us to where we are because he needs another storyteller for the folks who follow after us.

Sometimes You Lose a Turn on the Wheel of Fortune

A little church on a rural road in Indiana held to the Christmas tradition of the "Hanging of the Greens." It was rich with memories for the small congregation. One Christmas, the church went high tech to advertise the event. They rented a huge electric sign to put next to the road: "COME TO THE HANGING OF THE GREENS. REFRESHMENTS WILL BE SERVED."

> Our meaning comes from understanding our place in the mess.

What a great idea...except they were looking for a new pastor, and you can imagine the look of horror on the faces of the pastoral candidate and his wife, the Greens, as they drove up to the church.

Life doesn't always advertise what's in store for us. It just happens. It's like a contestant taking a spin on the TV show *Wheel of Fortune*. Not everyone wins a new car. Some come just this close by not finishing the word puzzle: S T U P _ D.

Maybe you've come just that close to your "fortune." But then you lost your turn, and you've been tempted to throw a giant, purple hissy fit. Hear Solomon's sage advice: "Whoever fears God will avoid all extremes" (Ecclesiastes 7:18). The road to the winner's circle isn't a racetrack; it's a two-way, 25-mile-per-hour cobblestoned road with a slew of stoplights, a construction zone or two, and one 85-year-old man practicing for his funeral procession by driving slower than a turtle on crutches with his left turn signal light on.

I love to hear my lifelong friend Talmadge Johnson tell the story of the grandpa who was late to his grandson's little league game. When he had taken his seat behind home base, he looked at the scoreboard. To his horror, his grandson's team was behind 54-0, and the grandson was sitting on the bench.

Hoping to bring a little encouragement, he walked over to the dugout, got his grandson's attention, and shouted, "Hang in there, son!" The little boy smiled and shouted back, "I will, Grandpa! We haven't been up to bat yet, but you just wait. We'll beat the socks off these guys!"

Let's not hold our artifacts too tightly. Stay in the game. It'll soon be our turn at bat.

Enter the Sanctuary at Your Own Risk

One Sunday morning, the priest noticed Little Johnny was staring up at the large plaque that hung in the foyer of the church. It was covered with names, and small American flags were mounted on either side of it. The seven-year-old had been staring at the plaque for some time, so the priest walked up, stood beside the boy, and said quietly, "Good morning, Little Johnny."

"Good morning, Father," replied the young man, still focused on the plaque. "Father Scott, what is this?" Little Johnny asked. "Well, son, it's a memorial to all the young men and women who died in the service." Soberly, they stood together, staring at the large plaque. Little Johnny's voice was barely audible when he asked, "Which service? The 9:45 or the 11:15?"

. . . .

6

Imbalance
Is Better Than
No Balance at All

Back when people spoke the King James language, one of the Bible greats said, "I have learned, in whatsoever state I am, therewith to be content" (Philippians 4:11 KJV). I don't know in what part of the country "Whatsoever" may be located, but we could drive through three different states and still look for it! And the older we get, the more convinced we are that getting across that border is more difficult than it seems. Golden-agers look for steadiness. It's not the big things that concern our senior minds and make us discontent. It's the little things, like shopping for a black, one-piece bathing suit with a wide enough skirt to cover the effects of those "Seniors' 2-4-2" buffets at the Golden Utensils restaurant on ladies' day.

Balance is the goal. Once we hit 70, contentment with our body—or anything else—becomes as unlikely as finding a 78 rpm recording of Bing Crosby singing rap songs. So we buy some new-fangled something to make us feel better about ourselves. We've made payments on the first cars, last semesters, and happy marriages of our descendants. Now we're determined to spend a little money on ourselves. Our time has come!

We get a diet soda and an ice cream bar from the fridge, push the leather recliner back, kick off our worn-to-the-bunions slippers, and watch silly-talking people sell fake diamonds and liver spot cream on TV infomercials. We don't know why we've tuned in or what we're looking for. We have most of what we need, but it still seems as if something's missing. So we look.

When we've reached the point where we need binoculars to read the warning message on a Metamucil bottle, it's tougher to sort the trash from the treasure. The bifocals of discontentment often distort our view.

Maybe you've been checking out garage sales, and when you got home you woke the wife to show her your finds. For some reason, she'd taken a rain check on getting up at dawn to tiptoe around rickety card tables in oil-smelling garages. Maybe you got back while she was still beauty-sleeping and set your prized garage sale find on the edge of the bed. "Twenty bucks," you boast. "I got this baby for twenty bucks!"

She squints at it. "What is it?" (Obviously, she's doesn't recognize a bargain when she sees one.)

"A combination TV-VCR—barely used," you gloat.

Then the dreaded words fall from her mouth, smoother than "I Can't Believe It's Not Butter" off a George Foreman grill. "Does it work?"

A pang of fear strikes. You summon hope and say, "Watch this!" Unplugging your digital alarm clock, which immediately flashes its familiar "12:00" display, you plug the 1980s combo into the wall socket by the nightstand.

After several minutes, a grayish, blurred image sneaks from the bowels of its plastic cabinet and smears itself across the dusty screen. Two minutes later, what looks like a 1950s Mighty Mouse cartoon in a dense fog slowly comes into focus. Then, the onscreen image suddenly reduces itself to a whitish dot no bigger than the eraser on a No. 2 pencil.

"Maybe the VCR works," the wife says with a forced smile. You quickly load your never-viewed *How to Build Your Own Deck* video into the slot and press play. Nothing. "Have you tried the rewind?" the wife asks sweetly. "Whaddaya want for 20 bucks?" you snort.

At the next garage sale, you set the TV-VCR on a rickety card table in your own oil-smelling garage and play *Gaither Homecoming* videos nonstop, hoping to draw a few generous Baptists. But you'll probably end up selling it to a Lutheran for $1.

You're out a few bucks, but it was worth it. You've learned a good lesson about buying things you don't need just because it seems like a bargain. Our senior years are a perfect time for us to learn how to balance wants and needs.

We've watched our share of talking heads on the news channel. We even remember a few "penny-saved-penny-earned" lectures from dear old dad. But living in these modern times, when all we have to do to get our money is to email the bank, has made us a little giddy.

One of the greatest quotes ever came from the lips of a wealthy financier who was asked how much money it would take to make him happy. He replied, "Just a little more."

If stockbrokers and financial planners can't help us figure out how to be content in a land of plenty, maybe we need to go back to the Book. Isaiah, the poet prophet, nailed it when he said, "Why spend money on what is not bread, and your labor on what does not satisfy? Listen, listen to me, and eat what is good, and you will

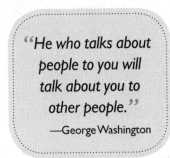

"He who talks about people to you will talk about you to other people."

—George Washington

delight in the richest of fare" (Isaiah 55:2). Random acts of spending won't fill the spiritual bare spots on the lawns of our heart.

Balanced living is more than matching the color of your purse with the color of your Crocs shoes. Let's examine it in light of Paul's letter to Christians in the New Testament book of Philippians, chapter 4.

A Happy Medium Is Rare, but It Can Be Well Done

"If anything is excellent or praiseworthy—think about such things" (Philippians 4:8). Balance begins in the mind even if the mind is a bit unbalanced. It's like the classic story of the man who strapped on his guitar, climbed a light pole by the county courthouse, and started singing "Don't Fence Me In."

The sheriff heard him, quickly ran outside, and demanded to know why he would do such a thing. The country star wannabe answered, "Well, it's like this, Sheriff. If I didn't do something stupid once in a while, I'd go crazy!"

"Excellent" in Paul's letter suggests a thoughtful restraint. In that light, balanced living is making thoughtful and restrained choices about:

- attitudes
- actions
- affections
- accumulations

And for the Christian, the gold standard is the behavior taught in God's Word, the Bible.

Attitudes impact actions, and actions impact affections. Let me illustrate that with a story I heard about a church business meeting. Now, as a pastor and church leader, I can assure you that a lot of church business meetings really aren't that funny. But this one deserves a hearing.

During the devotional time, right before the start of a church business meeting, one of the saints asked to say a word. Blubbering like a seal trying to whistle and rinse its mouth with Listerine at the same time, the lady president of the communion committee was recognized, and she began tearfully, "Y'all, I have a special prayer request. I really do need your prayers." She then began, "All week *(blubber)*...long, I've been *(wail)*...fighting the devil."

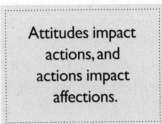

Attitudes impact actions, and actions impact affections.

Her husband was sitting beside her in the pew. As she went on, he began to slowly shake his head. Then he leaned over and whispered to a friend sitting next to him, loud enough to be heard two pews back, "All I got to say is, she ain't that easy to get along with either!"

We golden-agers often have more discretionary time and resources than we did when we started out. But with them, we have decisions to make about balance—decisions that affect behavior in these areas:

- entertainment
- thoughts and meditations
- reflections and attitudes
- time management
- stewardship of resources
- service to others
- relationships

Without balance, any of these areas can be jeopardized. I'd suggest putting balance decisions through the "Is it" checklist.

- Is it God-pleasing?
- Is it good for me?

- Is it good for my family and friends?

- Is it worthwhile?

I realize that's a pretty simple checklist, but I think it has merit in determining our direction and balance.

Copy the Best Practice of the Practicing

A pastor greeted folks as they left the service. Shaking one parishioner's hand, he said, "Edgar, good to see you. It's been a while. Have you been active in the service of the Lord?" The man replied, "Yes, sir. I have."

The pastor said, "Good. I've been a little worried. Ever since you joined the church, it seems like the only times I've seen you in the crowd are on Christmas and Easter."

Edgar replied, "I know it looks that way, Preacher, but I'm workin' undercover."

The apostle Paul wrote, "Whatever you have learned or received or heard from me, or seen in me—put it into practice" (Philippians 4:9). Achieving balance often means modeling the behavior of a significant person in your life who leads a balanced life. I've said many times that Dr. Melvin Maxwell, the father of my college classmate John C. Maxwell, had a GIANT influence on my life. He was definitely a follower of Christ who didn't work undercover. The godly way he planned, led, taught, and, most of all, lived taught me about a successful life.

Who comes to your mind right now who is living a balanced Christian life in old age? What are their priorities? How do they influence others? What motivates them? In what way do you need to be more like them?

You can balance your weakness with another's strength. Pick and choose. Do what you can, and *can* what you can't!

5 Steps to Solving Your Computer Problem

1. Call the mother of your grandchild and tell her about the computer problem.

2. Ask the mother if she could bring the grandchild over for a fellowship time.

3. While the grandchild is eating refreshments, lead her or him into the computer room.

4. Explain the problem to the grandchild and wait five minutes.

5. Thank the grandchild for solving the problem.

Hasty Actions Make Nasty Reactions

The pastor guided the seven-year-old candidate into the baptismal pool. "Your full name?" the pastor asked. He loudly responded, "Edward Jeffrey Charles Martin Mackenzie the Third!" From behind the platform, the custodian shouted, "Hold it, Preacher. I'll go get some more water!"

Golden-agers don't like surprises. Like Thoroughbred horses, when we become spooked, we sometimes kick up our heels. So when the meat of God's Word looks a little tough to chew, we have to take small bites (just like Mama said).

Here's a piece of sanctified steak served by Chef Paul: "I have learned to be content whatever the circumstances" (Philippians 4:11). Chomp...chomp...chomp! To be content when our Facebook account has been hacked? Or content when the folks in those big buildings in Washington talk about reducing our Social Security checks so they'll have more money to spend on that migration of mice program?

We don't have to be content with the actions of man; we have to be content with the will of God *through* the actions of man. "Let everyone be subject to the governing authorities, for there is no authority except that which God has established" (Romans 13:1). Sometimes God uses our sudden discontents for our long-range contentment.

A Christ-Controlled Life Is Remote Controlled

"I can do all this through him who gives me strength" (Philippians 4:13). Paul didn't have access to Wi-Fi, but he had something better. He had a dedicated line to the throne of God. He knew that a balanced life is a Christ-controlled life.

The situations or problems we try to solve on our own will never be as solvable as those that are solved by the leading of the

Holy Spirit. He is the ever-present connection to the mainframe of heaven. He not only has access to all the stored data of our lives, he also has a pop-up solution.

When we can't trust anything in life, we can trust him.

> **Sometimes God uses our sudden discontents for our long-range contentment.**

Slidin' Home

One of the responsibilities of the pastor in a funeral situation is to try to respect the wishes of the family. Naturally, when the funeral director advised me that the young granddaughter of the dearly departed wanted to sing during the graveside committal, I was happy to comply.

At the appropriate time in the service, I motioned to Nancy. The little girl bravely stood and walked to the end of the casket. Facing the rather large crowd huddled under the tent in the cemetery, she announced, "In Granny's honor, I'd like to sing a song she taught me." And then, as if she was performing with Carol Channing on Broadway, Nancy belted out several rounds of "Take Me Out to the Ballgame"!

I was next. A little lost for words, I simply said, "Friends, I can just see Granny looking over the railing in heaven's grandstand. Let's hear it for Nancy!"

The crowd then gave out a baseball cheer, with the whooping and hollering that would accompany a grand-slam home run.

I'm sure both Granny and Nancy were well pleased.

. . . .

7

If You Can't Keep Up with the Joneses, Park Your Shopping Cart

For some, life in the golden years means getting back to nature by camping in a diesel-powered motor home, watching the Travel Channel on a 50-inch smart TV, and waiting for a pizza delivery. But often, those "happy campers" are as miserable as a cat caught in a car wash.

Golden-agers grew up listening to how bad things either used to be or soon will be. So we overcompensate by buying stuff that will make us look richer, younger, thinner, and more secure than those who are half our age. Before the first Kardashian was born, our parents called it "keeping up with the Joneses."

Those of us without enough pain tolerance for liposuctions or Botox injections are left with so much flappage that taking a walk on a windy day may send us airborne. Or the water aerobics coach at the Monday Movement class tells us to take the water wings off our arms, and we aren't wearing any!

Golden-agers look for contentment by wearing *this*, having *that*, or doing *whatever*, only to end up on a cold metal chair in a Walmart fitting room. Let me explain.

The way I heard it, it all started when Uncle Frank and Aunt Helen took a forty-ninth anniversary outing to Walmart. Helen wanted Frank to buy a Speedo swimsuit like the Olympic diving team wears. She thought it would make him look younger and trimmer. Frank said by the time he wrestled that little swimsuit over his spare tire in a fitting room smaller than a porta-potty, he had an anxiety attack and had to sit on a cold metal chair. He added, "The goose bumps made me an inch taller!"

And don't think it's accidental that he couldn't see what he really looked like in that mirror on the wall. There wasn't enough light in that fitting room to give a sponge bath to a hippopotamus. Store managers know if people can't see themselves, they'll take a gamble on tiny swimsuits to divert attention from cellulite and spider veins.

> "Sometimes I lie awake at night and I ask, 'Where have I gone wrong?' Then a voice says to me, 'This is going to take more than one night.'"
>
> —Charlie Brown

The Bible says, "Keep your lives free from the love of money and be content with what you have" (Hebrews 13:5). The writer reminds us that contentment isn't found in a Dow Jones average or an upscale store catalog. Contentment is within reach. You can be as poor as a church mouse, rich as a royal, slim as a straw, tubby as a tuba, or happy as a clam, and still be as content as a Toler brother with an RC Cola and a moon pie in hand, watching a West Virginia football game!

And if your idea of eating out is sitting on the deck, sucking a SlimFast shake through a straw, remember, you've already done the young and trim thing in your high school graduation picture. Think of what the real young and trimmers have to look forward to! One day *they* will be gasping for breath in some fitting room, shivering on a cold metal chair, and wishing they hadn't chosen a swimsuit made for a pet hamster.

Contentment is a state of the heart that affects the mind. It comes from Matthew 6:33 thinking and doing: "Seek first his kingdom and his righteousness, and all these things will be given to you as well."

The Old Testament book of Judges gives us insights on contented and discontented living. Judges 11 focuses on discontent in the family of Jephthah, a warrior son of Gilead. Driven from the family circle by his ugly stepbrothers, and then recruited by them when they faced an enemy army, Jephthah learned to be content in a contentious culture.

Contentment Isn't Biological

Judges 11:2 reveals the family struggle: "'You are not going to get any inheritance in our family,' they said, 'because you are the son of another woman.'"

Jephthah was a brother by another mother. But instead of a common bond with his brothers, he had a broken relationship. Family jealousies caused discontent and separation, so the mighty warrior had to find contentment without sitting in the shade of the family tree. Not all family settings are like an episode of *Happy Days*. For example, a college president was invited to have dinner with a trustee board member's family, including their visiting five-year-old granddaughter.

This was a big moment for the trustee, whose term on the board was up for reelection that spring. His wife determined to pad her husband's chances with a fancy dinner and some intelligent conversation around the table.

The president finally arrived and was ushered into the living room. He was greeted enthusiastically by Schultz, the family dog—a Great Dane/Saint Bernard mix—who slapped his front paws over the president's shoulders, sending him flying...backwards...over an overstuffed footstool and into an antique rocker.

Embarrassed by the "dog gone wild" attack, the trustee muttered a few words about the weather and excused himself to help his wife in the kitchen and discuss a dog obedience course. When he left, the president tidied himself back up and tried to make conversation with the five-year-old. "What are we having for dinner tonight?" he asked. She shrugged her little shoulders and answered with raised eyebrows, "I'm not real sure, but I think it's mule."

"Mule!" the president gasped. "What makes you think we'll be having mule?"

"Well, last night I heard Grandpa and Grandma talking about you coming over, and Grandpa said, 'He's a stubborn ol' mule, but it's probably time we had him for supper.'"

Contentment Isn't Geographical

Jephthah got the hint and packed his overnight bag. "Jephthah fled from his brothers and settled in the land of Tob, where a gang of scoundrels gathered around him and followed him" (Judges 11:3). Notice how discouragement gathers a crowd!

I can't even begin to identify with that phase of Jephthah's story. My family's *bonds* have always been greater than its *stocks*. And adversity only strengthens them.

The Tolers weren't just raised in the poorest town of the poorest county in West Virginia; we were raised in obscurity. Santa didn't even have our address. We were born on the wrong side of the West Virginia mountains in an unincorporated coal mining camp called Baileysville. If I remember/exaggerate right, the economy was so depressed we couldn't even afford a crime rate.

Our family probably invented the expression, "If you can't stand the heat, get out of the living room." In the winter, our heating system was a potbellied stove in the basement that sent heat up through the floor vent. And in the summer, our cooling system was a mountain breeze sneaking through the gaps in the window frames.

Judge Your Worth by What's Not for Sale in Your Life

* Your house may be on the market, but your integrity isn't.

* You may be considering a vehicle trade-in, but you've determined to be faithful to your family.

* The interest rate on your mortgage may be negotiable, but your honesty is nonnegotiable.

* A job promotion may have a price tag, but you're not in the market.

* You have character, pride, and integrity. You're rich!

But contentment wasn't a big problem for the Tolers. We were loved, and we knew it! My dad was a coal miner by trade and a hero by his family's estimation, a man who worked hard to provide the best he could for us. He taught us by example to be good and godly men—a role I tried to assume at age 11 when he was killed in a work accident.

My precious mother raised three hyperactive boys when ADHD were just letters in a Scrabble game. She did it with a Bible, a well-worn paddle, and ever-loving arms. Mom would also gather us around a well-used upright piano with a few ivories that had expired during the last winter. There, we not only learned how to get along harmoniously, but we also learned to sing the four-part harmony that culminated in my brother Terry becoming a platinum award-winning songwriter, and all the brothers singing together in concerts and conferences across the nation.

One day when I was a youngster, a fire destroyed the Tolers' little white house on Baileysville Mountain. I was crushed, but my dad turned it into a life lesson as he did many things. I saw him put his arm around our pastor, who had rushed to the scene, and tell him, "The Lord gave, and the Lord hath taken away; blessed be the name of the Lord." (See Job 1:21 KJV.) I learned the true meaning of contentment on that day. It wasn't based on what material things we wanted. It was based on what we already had: one another and faith in a God who kept his promises.

We can't put Contentment in our GPS and get to its destination. We train to be content in God's immediate provision.

Contentment Isn't Situational

Verses 5-6 of Judges 11 are interesting: "The elders of Gilead went to get Jephthah from the land of Tob. 'Come,' they said, 'be our commander.'" The family that wasn't happy until they got rid of

Jephthah soon wasn't happy till they got him back! I can't imagine Jephthah being comfortable with the offer or returning to the guest list for the family picnic of those who delisted him for not bringing angel food cake to the last picnic. But contentment doesn't come with an invitation we've looked forward to receiving.

> We can't put Contentment in our GPS and get to its destination.

Maxie Dunnam wrote about the elderly man who began spending time with an elderly woman from the man's church. They both were unclaimed door prizes in the senior social circle, but each time they were together, the gentleman recognized a growing attachment to the lady. The problem was, he was too nervous to admit it and too shy to say it.

After many days of anxiety over hidden feelings that kept resurfacing, he finally got nerve enough to stake a claim. Without any courtship experience, he simply went over to her house unannounced, asked her to sit with him on the orthopedic porch swing, and blurted out like an announcer on *The Price is Right*, "Miss Shirley, let's get married!"

Miss Shirley's eyes widened. She inhaled deeply and replied, "Why, that's a splendid idea. I've been thinking that same thing. But at our age, who in the world would have us?"

Maybe you've had a different letdown. Maybe you've been looking somewhere else, thinking, *If only I*_____ (fill in the blank). For golden-agers, discontent is often as common as age spots. Whether it comes from a financial uncertainty, post-traumatic retirement syndrome, aches and pains, or the changing environment of a society moving faster than we are, in our golden years we often feel an emotional gap.

So we often try to fill the gap with cruises, gadgets, hobbies, or three-wheeled motorcycles. But the luster often fades faster than cheap eyeliner in a rainstorm.

Deep-down, mind-settling contentment doesn't come from a profession, a possession, or a relocation. It comes with thankfulness for what we have and where it came from.

Contentment Isn't Logical

"Jephthah went with the elders of Gilead, and the people made him head and commander over them" (Judges 11:11). The unwanted warrior suddenly was as popular as an overscouted, seven-foot-tall basketball player who is thinking about skipping his senior year of high school. Have you ever met someone in the *least* likely vocation, location, or situation say, "I've never been happier in my life"? Contentment doesn't always make sense. It goes against the laws of the natural and hangs its hat on the spiritual.

Ask the apostle John. Dumped like a former vice president onto the deserted island of Patmos by the haters of everything he was or stood for, John found it to be a niche. Instead of complaining to the Patmos visitor's bureau, he pulled out his laptop, sat under a tree with a coconut-shaped glass of sweet tea, and started writing about heaven.

Fact is, he wasn't really alone. The Friend of the friendless took up residence with him, whispering promises into his contented heart and taking him on side trips to Glory during a break in his writing.

Contentment at any age starts and ends with a *who*, not a *what* or *where*! (And you-know-who is the Who!)

Man's Best Friend and His Faith

Old Muldoon lived alone in the Irish countryside with only his pet dog to keep him company.

One sad day, Muldoon's beloved dog died, and Muldoon went to the parish priest and said, "Father Patrick, my dog is dead. Could ya' be sayin' a mass for the poor creature?"

Father Patrick understood Old Muldoon's grief but had to answer, "I'm afraid not. We cannot be havin' services for an animal in the church. But there is a denomination down the lane, and there's no tellin' what they believe. Maybe they'll do somethin' for the poor creature."

Old Muldoon replied, "Bless you, Father. I'll go right away." But before he walked off, he stopped and asked, "Do ya' think $5,000 is enough to pay for their services?"

Father Patrick threw his arms around the poor bereaved Muldoon and exclaimed, "Sweet Mary, Mother of Jesus, come inside, my good friend. Why didn't ya tell me the dog was Catholic?"

. . . .

8

It's Hard to Be Positive When You're Chasing Pigs

A friend of mine married a lovely lady who was raised on a small farm in the Midwest. He said, fortunately, by the time he arrived to "set her heart on fire with a perfect match," the cows had been sold. But he said there was a small-but-smelly herd of hogs housed in their state-of-the-art barn. Unfortunately, on one weekly visit to the lovely lady on the farm, there was an incident.

The little pigs had an "oinkling" that they were going to market, so they had a midnight conference and voted to escape. When my friend arrived, his sweetheart and her family were running around the front yard as though they were being chased by killer bees, but actually they were chasing pigs.

He said he got a crash course in pig chasing that day. He told me, "There was hollering. There were threats. There was even some talk of a pig roast." He also said he missed more tackles than a third-string lineman on a JV football team who was so surprised when the coach told him to get in the game that he put his helmet on backwards.

Living in the senior years is a lot like trying to maintain a positive attitude when your helmet is on backwards and you're chasing pigs that are running in more directions than an Independent campaigning for governor.

Maybe some unexpected things in your life got loose and are running through your yard, trampling down your positive mental attitude along the way. What to do? You just have to believe that you'll win the chase. Combining past victories with expecting a good outcome is the only way to survive.

Some of the "pigs" running loose are very real. Others are imaginary. Some are even inherited. Chances are, if one or more of our kin is a member of Worriers Anonymous, we'll break out in a cold fret now and then. But remember, negative is not just the opposite of positive—it's the opposite of faith. The writer of the book of Hebrews said, "Faith is confidence in what we *hope* for and *assurance* about what we do not see" (Hebrews 11:1, emphasis added).

> But remember, negative is not just the opposite of positive—it's the opposite of faith.

What's Your Stress Size?

The great apostle Paul would have made Norman Vincent Peale look like the chairman of Pessimist International! He faced snakes, shipwrecks, and Sadducees with a belief that God was in control of the situation. But once in a while, even Paul had to take his attitude to the Faith Shop to have his stress altered. Look at Acts 17:16: "While Paul was waiting for them in Athens, he was greatly distressed to see that the city was full of idols."

While waiting for the rest of his mission team to join him, Paul noticed that the Athenians had turned their religious ideas into idols. His temporary negative was a sanctified anger that sprang from their idolatry. In light of his devotion to Christ and the gospel, that wasn't cool.

Paul was human, like a lot of people, and he had a factory-installed boiling point. This time, Paul's boiling point was the godlessness in Athens, but sometimes boiling points are reached without such a holy zeal.

A pastor friend of mine told me about making an unexpected call to a member family's house that had more boil in it than Yellowstone Park's Old Faithful.

Sitting in the living room with the husband, he heard the sound of an overhead door opening in the garage. "There's my wife now," the husband announced. "She's been to the grocery store, spending my hard-earned money."

Meanwhile, the couple's precocious only child decided to play a trick on Mommy. As his mother tried to enter the kitchen door with her arms full of grocery bags, sonny boy put his five-year-old weight against the door. The harder she pushed, the harder he pushed.

My friend said the frustrated mother suddenly let out a string of cuss words that would embarrass a heathen sailor. "You stupid (blankety blank)! Open this (blankety blank) door right this (blankety blank) minute!"

Sheepishly, the embarrassed husband turned to my pastor friend and said, "I'll bet the missus is gonna be surprised to see you, Reverend."

No, we probably won't end up in that eternal place without air-conditioning with a boilover—and we may not be using blankety blanks—but we must come to terms with the fact that "distemper" is not only bad for dogs, it's bad for human attitudes. Looking at golden-ager situations with an "I thought so" or "I told you so" (or worse) attitude won't make our breakfast Cheerios swim in a smiley face formation.

> *"Irving Benson and Jessie Carter were married on October 24 in the church. So ends a friendship that began in their school days."*
> —Church announcement

And if we expect a worm in every apple, we'll probably find a few, but that doesn't mean the whole bushel is bad. It just means we have a tendency to get worms—a lingering negativity.

If It Weren't for People...

About the time the sailing turned smooth on the gospel ship in Athens, a few passengers on board threw a *Titanic*-sized party on the top deck. "A group of Epicurean and Stoic philosophers began to debate with him. Some of them asked, 'What is this babbler trying to say?'" (Acts 17:18).

Do you have any Epicureans and Stoic philosophers in your church? Most churches have a few. If it weren't for people, it would be a lot easier to have a positive attitude.

I once wrote about a time when an Epicurean incident put a crimp in my positive attitude. When three independent-thinking brothers sat in one short pew, you can be sure they weren't always singing "Blest Be the Tie That Binds"! The Toler brothers would often play tic-tac-toe on tithing envelopes during the church service, but one time the game turned to hangman!

I noticed that brother Terry and brother Mark were "taking sermon notes" on the envelopes when all of a sudden, there was conflict. Mark had a whispered debate with Terry. Terry would probably deny any

> *"Neither one of us can hear anymore, so it makes no sense to argue."*
>
> Answer given by a couple when asked for their secret to a 75-year marriage

wrongdoing, but we both will gladly verify that our little brother Mark had a king-sized carnal spell. He threw his pencil on the floor, wadded up his tithe envelope, and prepared to put a few stars in Terry's crown.

The posturing must have been obvious because all of a sudden

Mark felt an enormous pressure on the back of his neck (in that part where the top of the neck meets the bottom of the skull). Dad and Mom were sitting in the pew behind us, and Dad wanted to get a point across about church behavior. He did it with a flick of the finger that nearly pointed its way through Mark's skin.

Mark had what he would later call a near-death experience. He claims he entered into the heavens and saw two angels, three Old Testament prophets, Billy Sunday, D.L. Moody, Granny, and an uncle whose presence there would be a surprise to the whole family.

What's New Is an Old Problem

New stuff sometimes tips the recliner for us golden-agers. We feel a lot like the Epicureans and Stoics in Acts 17:20: "You are bringing some strange ideas to our ears, and we would like to know what they mean." New ideas sometimes give us hives! For example, about the time we learned how to use an electric typewriter, an "Apple" fell from a computer tree. And suddenly, it's "strange idea" time.

I heard a true story about an executive in his late middle age whose administrative assistant came into his office and found him with a computer mouse in hand, trying to erase a typo on the monitor screen of his first computer.

We've had to learn a whole new technical vocabulary:

- bytes
- bits
- gigs
- java
- malware
- server
- mainframe

Seniors Texting Code

~~~~~~

- ATD: At the doctor's
- BFF: Best friend fell
- BTW: Bring the wheelchair
- BYOT: Bring your own teeth
- FWIW: Forgot where I was
- GGPBL: Gotta go, pacemaker battery low
- GHA: Got heartburn again
- IMHO: Is my hearing aid on?
- LMDO: Laughing my dentures out
- OMSG: Oh my! Sorry, gas.
- TTYL: Talk to you louder
- ROFLACGU: Rolling on floor laughing and can't get up

There were probably times when we wanted to pick up a flash drive and throw it through the windows and then go someplace and hibernate until we could refresh enough to face our new virtual reality!

Positively Negative

Paul disarmed the negative nay bobs with a powerful positive: "People of Athens! I see that in every way you are very religious" (Acts 17:22). Looking on the bright side won't hurt us unless we look directly at the sun. In fact, it not only helps us, but it also brightens the day of the negative masses around us.

I heard of a retiree who had a case of the negatives, and he told his wife that his joint pain was getting so bad he wouldn't be able to do any manual labor around the house. She would have to take care of it.

When he met his buddy at Starbucks the next day, he told him about the conversation and his condition: "Yeah, it's so bad I had to cut my golf games back to just four days a week, and then I only have strength enough to play 18 holes!"

That would be a tough sell to our brave soldiers who get on with their lives after suffering terrible war wounds. YouTube had a video of a double amputee taking a bungee jump in his wheelchair. Bungee jump! I know folks who are so negative they wouldn't jump on one of those backyard trampolines without a parachute! They need a refresher course in *positive*.

> The true victory of old age is learning how to turn *setbacks* into *stairways*.

Actually, we were born positive. At birth, we had zero negative thoughts. Nine months indoors (in a flooded basement) was incentive enough to expect some sunshine in our life. Then, some negatives crept into the delivery room. After an impolite slap, someone grabbed a pair of scissors and cut our supply line. Ten months or so later, we had to learn how to carry our own weight (and the longer we live, the more weight we'll probably have to carry).

Of course, we will receive promotions along the way, but there'll be a few setbacks as well. Here's a Toler recipe for facing them:

- Evaluate their impact prayerfully.
- Compare their strength to God's power immediately.
- Search for and claim a Bible promise diligently.
- Surrender their outcome to God's will completely.

The true victory of old age is learning how to turn *setbacks* into *stairways*. And the best way to build a stairway is to enlist the aid of the Carpenter of Nazareth. If he can build mountains and then turn them into meadows, he can lead us up and down the inclines and valleys that life brings our way. And if he can build invisible fences around the seven seas, he can protect us when the storms come along to rock our boat.

Most of the time, Paul was either facing the rigors of leading or the rants of the followers, but we'll always find him taking a pause for an undignified "Hallelujah!" Here's one: "To him who is able to do immeasurably more than all we ask or imagine, according to his power that is at work within us, to him be glory in the church and in Christ Jesus throughout all generations, for ever and ever! Amen" (Ephesians 3:20-21).

Discipline Your Thought Life

- If you keep a tight grip on your thoughts, you'll be less likely to lose control of your life.

- Refuse to do things in your mind that you would never do in real life.

- Refuse to let inappropriate thoughts stay long enough to get comfortable.

- Refuse to imagine rude or demeaning thoughts about others.

- Refuse to fantasize about living a lifestyle you know is not truly you.

Everybody can be great because any-body can serve. You don't have to have a college degree to serve. You don't have to make your subject and your verb agree to serve. You only need a heart full of grace, a soul generated by love.

—Martin Luther King Jr.

. . . .

9

Is There a Topical Cream for Worry Warts?

Twenty-first-century living can be as encouraging as an oil change at a Fast Oil business. About ten minutes into the process, a sad-faced young mechanic will walk slowly to the waiting room (that has all the ambience of a deserted airport in the Sahara Desert) with a flashlight and an air filter in his greasy hand. He'll tap you on your arm that's holding a filled-to-the-brim cup of boiling-hot, machine-made coffee and point the flashlight toward the air filter.

His next words start the worry warts a growin': "Us folks at Fast Oil think your air filter should be changed every two months or less, but this'n looks like it ain't been changed in, like, forever, man." He won't look you in the eye because he knows the new $30 filter only costs $.50 to produce and was manufactured by a robot that didn't get a dime.

When the golden years are dawning, we worry about different stuff than we did when our twenties were roaring. For example, the surprise pregnancy announcement

> When the golden years are dawning, we worry about different stuff than we did when our twenties were roaring.

you got the week after you celebrated your fourth child's second birthday is in the past (though you should remember the biblical

Sarah got a passing grade on her pregnancy test when she was just a tad past 90!).

Anxiety is a rite of passage for many golden-agers. And if someone discovers a topical cream for worry warts, they'll make more money than an ambidextrous knuckleball pitcher in the big leagues.

> "God, grant me the serenity to accept the things I cannot change, the courage to change the things I can, and the wisdom to know the difference."
>
> —Reinhold Niebuhr

Maybe there aren't more things to worry about now than there were in the '50s, but thanks to social media, it just seems like it. For instance, a blogger can write a hundred words on the dangers of licking the kitchen knife after spreading peanut butter on a cracker, and a million people will repost it on the internet and send it to five family members without knowing whether said blogger has even finished preschool!

Elijah the prophet was not only known for his forth-telling skills, but he was also known for getting the glums and occasional worry. We catch up to him as he gets his woes in a row after being threatened with death by Queen Jezebel for putting 450 false prophets out of work permanently (know what I mean?).

You Have "Flees" In Your Running Shoes

First Kings 19:3 says, "Elijah was afraid and ran for his life." Worry and fear are first cousins on their father the devil's side. And the events that sent the prophet to the sporting goods store for a new pair of running shoes meant the cousins would ride along.

I'll admit there are some things that can keep us on the run and wishing we were living on Gold Mountain Road in heaven. Here are a few legit worries.

1. *Physically,* once we enter our golden years we spend so much time at the drugstore, pharmacy schools want to name buildings after us. It's as though the lost medical tribes of the Old Testament have camped in our backyard:

- The Rheumatoids
- The Tendonitisites
- The Cataracttites
- The Indigestionenes
- The Insomniabeds
- The Bladderthons

And the *Massophysicians* came with them, setting up quick clinics in their motor homes.

When my senior years dawned, I had to face the new reality. I could still jump out of bed in the morning, but joint pains chased me all the way to the bathroom and stayed there till I finished my shower. Knowing I had finally qualified to be a golden-ager, one of my goals was to eliminate the maladies of my brothers and sisters who weren't stopped for going over 50 in a twenty-first-century speed zone. I know I can't, so all I can do is offer some proven instructions.

2. *Financially,* golden-agers worry that bulls and bears are playing hide-and-seek in their stock portfolios. The financial times are about as steady as Dean Martin after a pizza party at Frank Sinatra's house.

The apostle Peter gives us some certified financial counsel: "In his great mercy, he has given us new birth into a living hope through the resurrection of Jesus Christ from the dead, and into an inheritance that can never perish, spoil or fade. This inheritance is kept in heaven for you, who through faith are shielded by God's power until the coming of the salvation that is ready to be revealed in the last time" (1 Peter 1:3-5). You can take that to the bank!

3. *Psychologically,* golden-agers are trying to forget what we had to overcome to get to where we're going. The past may have been this tough:

- Your winters were so cold you had to put jumper cables on your toaster. And summers were so short that by the time you changed into short sleeves, it was time for long underwear.
- The combined income of your parents and seven siblings wasn't enough to buy tennis shoes for a termite.
- You only had two milk cows. One was dry, and the other only gave skim milk because of a gastrointestinal blockage.

4. *Socially,* we are trying to treat our friends and loved ones as though we are on an episode of *Leave It to Beaver*, and everyone in the next generation thinks we're talking about an animal documentary on the public broadcasting station. We have to relearn our social skills:

- Pictures have replaced words.
- Best friendships sometimes have term limits.
- Absolutes are considered to be relative.
- Loyalty is tenuous and largely ignored.

How to Live Right

- *Eat right*—Feed your body with the right foods, and your soul with God's Word.

- *Think right*—Focus on the pure instead of the perverted.

- *Do right*—Live above prejudice and vengeance by totally loving God and others.

- *Be right*—Be more concerned with your own character than the conduct of others.

- *Talk right*—Determine to be on the positive and bright side of the conversation.

- *Act right*—Show your allegiance to God with godly behavior.

- *Look right*—Keep your eyes on the hope of Christ's coming instead of the horrors of current events.

- Change is a given.

- Compassion is often social-issue related.

One of my favorite relational stories is about a pastor in Mississippi who discovered a dead mule in the back of the church parking lot. He called the local sheriff to report it. The sheriff recommended that he call the health department. The health director said to call the sanitation department. The sanitation director told the pastor he needed the mayor's authorization.

> "You can tell more about a person by what he says about others than you can by what others say about him."
> —Leo Aikman

The mayor must have just received word that his salary had been reduced due to budget cuts, so he was in a sarcastic mood when the preacher called. "Preacher, isn't it your job to bury the dead?"

Exhausted by the runaround, the preacher said, "Yes, sir. But right now I'm just notifying the next of kin."

Worry is a perceived inadequacy in yourself or your situation that notifies its next of kin, the spirit, making it the caretaker of its condition.

God is a better Caretaker. "The LORD is my strength and my shield; my heart trusts in him, and he helps me" (Psalm 28:7).

Once, when my brother Terry was trying to preach, a little boy in the front row was racing toy cars on the pew. That wasn't so bad (it kept him from writing on the tithing envelopes), but the little boy suddenly started making engine noises to go along with it, "VROOM! VROOM! VROOM! VROOM!" Seeing it was disturbing those near the little boy, Terry stopped the sermon and said playfully, "Son, you think we should put the brakes on that car?" The little boy quickly responded—with an even louder sound effect: "SCREEEECH!"

Maybe you've had to hit the brakes a few times. Before you add the memory of those times to a permanent worry list, remember that God maps both the coming and the going. "You have rescued me from death; you have kept my feet from slipping. So now I can walk in your presence, O God, in your life-giving light" (Psalm 56:13 NLT).

Angels in the Room

Verses 4 and 5 of 1 Kings 19 are quite revealing. Elijah prayed, "'Take my life; I am no better than my ancestors.' Then he lay down under the bush and fell asleep." All at once an angel touched him. Nearly every parent knows that heart-stopping moment when they are sound asleep and suddenly wake up to their child standing over their bed nearly face-to-face with them. That'll beat a stress test in the best hospital in Dallas by a country mile!

Elijah had wearily reached the end of his stress rope, and he asked God to take his life. God's solution was reminiscent of the gospel song "Angels in the Room." God always has a representative at the scene of our restlessness. When life puts on the brakes, God shows us a passing lane.

> God always has a representative at the scene of our restlessness.

Fastest Food Delivery

I like the TV commercial that features an elderly man sitting in an overstuffed chair, using a touch-tone phone to call Jimmy John's for a sub. Before he even hangs up the phone, a delivery boy bursts into the room with the sandwich. The old man's response suggests his backache was playing tag with his gout: "What took you so long?" Elijah's food delivery was even faster: "He looked around, and there by his head was some bread baked over hot coals, and a jar of water" (1 Kings 19:6). Did you catch that? God sent bottled water along with the sandwich! He always adds value to our requests.

God Left the Light On

I like the story of the man who was ushered through the pearly gates to a registration table with an angel behind it, checking folks in. As he approached the table, he started to give his name. The angel interrupted him, saying, "No need for that, Bill. We know who you are and what you've done. There's only one little bit of information we don't have in our files."

Feeling a bit nervous, Bill asked, "And what can that be?"

The angel replied, "Well, we know you bravely rescued a driver from being pursued by an outlaw biker gang. And we know that when you stood between the bikers and the driver, you courageously said, 'C'mon, you bunch of wimps! I can beat the daylights out of any or all of you!' What we're missing is the exact time when all of this occurred, and we wondered if you might help us."

"Sure," Bill replied as he looked down at his new gold watch and thought out loud. "It happened...oh, I'd say about 30 seconds ago."

We don't know the specifics on the rest of Elijah's night or what he had for breakfast the next morning, but we do know that he continued on his journey, probably with shoulders bent over, plodding

> "When you stop giving and offering something to the rest of the world, it's time to turn out the lights."
> —George Burns

along like Eeyore until he reached a motel, where God had left the light on. "He went into a cave and spent the night. And the word of the Lord came to him" (1 Kings 19:9).

We can count on taking this to the bank: When worries overtake us, God will provide a resting place—and turn on the light of his Word.

I like to think of the book of Psalms as God's five-star accommodations, where we check in to find a bottle of refreshing, cool water on the nightstand. Here, have a few sips.

7 Ways to Face the Day

1. *With gratitude* that God will always provide for you: "I will say of the Lord, 'He is my refuge and my fortress, my God, in whom I trust'" (Psalm 91:2).

2. *With trust* in God's authority over those who govern you: "It is better to take refuge in the Lord than to trust in princes" (Psalm 118:9).

3. *With confidence* that God's supply for you will never run out: "Those who know your name trust in you, for you, Lord, have never forsaken those who seek you" (Psalm 9:10).

4. *With reliance* on God's wisdom and strength for your daily tasks: "Commit everything you do to the Lord. Trust him, and he will help you" (Psalm 37:5 NLT).

5. *With understanding* that God will never stop loving you: "Give thanks to the God of gods. His love endures forever" (Psalm 136:2).

6. *With resolve* to see God's redeeming work in the events of your days: "Let the one who is wise heed these things and ponder the loving deeds of the Lord" (Psalm 107:43).

7. *With joy* that God will honor your trust and obedience: "The blameless spend their days under the LORD's care, and their inheritance will endure forever" (Psalm 37:18).

No matter where we are on our journey, we're just visiting. Let's make the most of every moment, say the best of every person, and see the positive in every situation.

Barbara C. remains in the hospital and needs blood donors for more transfusions. She is also having trouble sleeping and requests tapes of Pastor Jack's sermons.

Notice in church bulletin

. . . .

It always looks the darkest right before it gets totally black.

Charlie Brown

. . . .

10

Does This Bible Make Me Look Too Young?

I learned about service during the service. That is, I learned about serving the Lord growing up, but my training went into speed mode when I preached my first sermon. I don't remember which Bible I was holding, but for the first few minutes it felt bigger than one of those coffee table–sized family Bibles that are big enough to hold an entire family tree.

Back then, most preachers had a Bible in hand as they preached, and sometimes they held it up for emphasis. On that Sunday, ratio-wise, the Bible probably made me look like an actor in *Honey, I Shrunk the Kids*. Some probably said I was too young for the assignment, but God didn't see it that way. A pulpit needed filling, and he decided to use me as an object lesson to prove that anyone of any age could do what needs to be done.

That belt buckle line is a reminder of the fickle fashions of yesterday and today. If we're going to snicker at today's adolescent fashions (or lack thereof), we'll need to remember the "in" look in our own teen years: guys in pegged-leg pants that looked as though they were duct taped at the cuff, and gals in large, hooped skirts that looked like opened parachutes with poodle dog silhouettes sewn on them.

Sad to say, I took that look into the pulpit as a 14-year-old preacher! But as I've grown older and wiser, I've begun to realize that "in" doesn't have a specific look or even an age limit.

We don't know the fashion style when Moses was a teen, but

Top 10 Indications
You're a Redneck Preacher

10. If your "Sunday school bus" is a tractor and hay wagon.

9. If you've ever had someone bid on the livestock during the Christmas program.

8. If the middle name of your entire church board is "Bob."

7. If your preaching robe has pockets to hold your cell phone and duct tape.

6. If your church directory has 150 families (with a combined total of 90 teeth).

5. If you've ever taken a possum casserole to a shut-in.

4. If your worship leader uses "I'm Glad to Be an American" as an invitation song.

3. If you have to announce, "No more making change in the offering plate."

2. If you've ever held your Valentine's Day dinner at Waffle House.

1. If your belt buckle is bigger than your Bible.

(Mark Hollingsworth and Stan Toler)

somewhere along the journey he stopped by heaven's outlet store and picked out a robe of righteousness. Later on, to complete the look, he would hold a staff in his hand that was so tall it reached all the way to heaven and back.

Like many of us, Moses struggled with the call of God on his life; he had some self-image problems. But when he turned 80, during a bonfire service in the desert—with nobody else there to join him in singing "Kum Ba Ya, My Lord" ("Come by Here, My Lord"), the Lord actually came by, and you might say held Moses's feet to the fire (see Exodus 3:1-9). The reaction of Moses to God's call is an awesome lesson.

Sitting on the Premises

After God gave Moses a history lesson, he gave him a homework assignment. "Now, go. I am sending you" (Exodus 3:10). God is always on the move, so I guess he expects his followers to be in motion as well. We are called to:

- stand up
- stand out
- stand for
- stand against

We may be "standing on the promises," but we have to make decisions about what's next: sitting on the premises or participating in the services.

While leading a business meeting in South America, I was trying to give my official greetings in Spanish. Suddenly, a chicken invaded the outdoor auditorium and took a surprise lap around the seating area. I guess the ol' bird got such a kick out of the greeting that she dashed into the auditorium and started running around to see who was talking.

> When God calls us to do something, he doesn't look back at our bumbling. He focuses on our new beginnings.

A bunch of dignitaries tried, but none seemed to be able to shoo her away. In fact, a little while later the hilarious hen came back for a second lap. I maintained my official decorum until she came to a complete stop in front of the podium and raised her head up toward me, as if to say, "Was that you? You must have learned Spanish from a home study course bought off a shopping channel on German TV."

The score was Chicken–1; General Superintendent–0.

Maybe you haven't been outsmarted by a South American chicken, but you've had humbling moments:

- You've been to a formal occasion and suddenly realized you were wearing a brown shoe on your left foot and a black shoe on the right.

- You've been in a hurry and were next in a long line at the "12 Items or Less" counter of Walmart; you put your 22 items on the moving belt but forgot to bring your wallet (or purse).

- You've brought guests to a restaurant, and when you left, you tried desperately to unlock a car in the parking lot that wasn't even yours.

When God calls us to do something, he doesn't look back at our bumbling. He focuses on our new beginnings.

"You Got the Wrong Idiot"

I like the story of the lady who fought insomnia with a sleeping pill and had finally gone to sleep when her cell phone on the bedroom dresser started ringing at four o'clock in the morning.

When she answered half awake, the caller said, "Is this Pizza Hut?" The woman, thoroughly aggravated, hollered into the phone, "You got the wrong idiot, you number!"

Exodus 3:4 says, "God called to him [Moses] from within the bush." Fully awake, Moses must have felt like that lady. "Who am I that I should go?" (Exodus 3:11). Moses had some serious reservations about his qualifications, just like we've had on some occasions.

"Show 'Em Your Card."

When Moses pondered his call to service, he thought about the assignment, the people, and his credentials. God knew his thoughts. "This is what you are to say to the Israelites: 'I AM has sent me to you'" (Exodus 3:14).

You've probably heard the classic story about the county officer checking whether dog owners had licenses for their dogs. Walking up to a porch and noticing a dog chain wrapped around the rocker of a chair filled with a crusty member of the seniors bowling league, he said, "Mornin,' sir. You got a dog?" The ol' fella replied nonchalantly, "Yep."

A bit put off at the response, the officer pulled out a business card and showed it to the man. "Sir, I'm an officer of the county, and I'm here to check on dog licenses. May I see your dog?"

"He's in the house," the man replied. "G'wan up to the door, but I'd be careful if I was you."

The county officer boldly marched to the screen door and started to open it. Suddenly, a pit bull mix burst through the bottom screen of the door in full attack mode, its mouth wide open, foam dripping, and teeth bared as if he was about to tear an arm and a leg off an intruder.

The dog owner lumbered toward the vicious attack, grabbed the dog by its straining collar, and hollered over the barking, "Guess you better show him that business card!"

I don't have an official "Grandpa" card, but I am a practicing grandfather ("Pookie" as I'm known in my grandkids' circle), and I love it! A while after I started making toy store stops in airports, God even photoshopped my hair and took out the color so I could officially join my fellow grandpas in showing grandchild pics on our smartphones.

Golden-agers have certified experience and God-given opportunities that provide added value to their lives. We have learned people and character skills that last for life and are transferable to the next generation.

"For Here or To Go?"

Since we've watched *The Ten Commandments* on TV, obviously Moses (not Charlton Heston) settled his service contract issues with the Lord. And God followed that up with an ongoing supply contract that had the power of his name behind it. "This is my name forever...from generation to generation" (Exodus 3:15).

"Chronic chronology"—the onset of aging—doesn't have to be defined in how many positions we can adjust our La-Z-Boy without falling out. It can be defined by agreeing with God that we can fill a need by letting the "ice" melt and putting the "serve" back in "service." God never takes back his gifts. They may need an upgrade, but they're still under warranty.

The Medicare years can be bad for our health. With "six Saturdays and a Sunday" of retirement, it's possible to cocoon and let the butterflies wing it.

I heard the story of a golden-aged worker who became an assistant chef in a restaurant partly to learn a new trade, and partly to get out of the house while her husband watched live sports events streamed to the TV in his man cave.

Because she took leftovers home to her husband (who would take nourishment during rain delays, replays, halftimes, or seventh-inning stretches), she asked a vendor about the vegetables he brought. "Sir, I'm responsible for taking leftover food home to my husband, who sits in front of the TV set *all day* watching sports! Are you *absolutely sure* life-threatening chemicals are not on these vegetables?"

The kindly young vendor said, "No, ma'am. There aren't any life-threatening chemicals on our vegetables. I'm afraid you'll have to add them yourself."

> "I know God will not give me anything I can't handle. I just wish that he didn't trust me so much."
>
> —Mother Teresa

There's more to life than streaming TV. People in Bible times were active into their hundreds (one even into the nine hundreds). Check them out:

- Methuselah served God for 969 years. Before they lit the candles on his retirement cake, the volunteer fire department had to be called in.

- Noah cleaned the stalls of two elephants in the basement of a houseboat without windows or room deodorizer for a year on a Mediterranean cruise ship.

- Enoch power walked with such determination that he walked all the way to heaven before he knew it.

- The Abrahams (Old Testament "oldyweds") started a

family that, so far, has grown to more than two billion members.

Who knows what you or I could do if we determined to put our gifts back in service! Why, the Holy Spirit can give us so much strength, we could lift an entire religious organization up to God from a kneeling position!

Following are seven reasons why we should take up the torch of service and put a fire under our feet:

1. *We have positive characteristics that no other person has.* "Shall what is formed say to the one who formed it, 'Why did you make me like this?'" (Romans 9:20).

2. *We have gifts and abilities that no other person has.* "Do not neglect your gift, which was given you through prophecy when the body of elders laid their hands on you" (1 Timothy 4:14).

3. *We have people who care for us more than anyone else in the world.* "We ought always to thank God for you, brothers and sisters loved by the Lord, because God chose you as firstfruits to be saved through the sanctifying work of the Spirit and through belief in the truth" (2 Thessalonians 2:13).

4. *We have an influence in someone's life that no one else has.* "About your love for one another we do not need to write to you, for you yourselves have been taught by God to love each other. And in fact, you do love all of God's family" (1 Thessalonians 4:9-10).

5. *We have life opportunities that no one else has.* "God is faithful, who has called you into fellowship with His Son, Jesus Christ our Lord" (1 Corinthians 1:9).

6. *We have people who depend on us more than anyone else.* "God is not unjust; he will not forget your work and the love you have shown him as you have helped his people and continue to help them" (Hebrews 6:10).

7. *We have a life story that is unique from that of any other person.* "God has placed the parts in the body, every one of them, just as he wanted them to be. If they were all one part, where would the body be? As it is, there are many parts, but one body" (1 Corinthians 12:18-20).

God determined that in some situations and for some people, only we could make a difference. So he gave us a totally unique life story. Some of the chapters were painful—because others need to know how to live with their own pain. Some of the chapters were delightful—because others need to know how to enjoy life. Some of the chapters were puzzling—because others need to know how to put the pieces of their life back together. Some of the chapters were eventful—because others need to know how to go through life-changing situations.

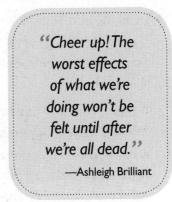

"Cheer up! The worst effects of what we're doing won't be felt until after we're all dead."
—Ashleigh Brilliant

Everything we have experienced or will experience is a life lesson for others. And our story will be told and retold years after we have taken a giant leap off planet Earth.

Can I get a "GO, BUBBA! YOU DA MAN!"?

About the Author

Stan Toler has spoken in over 90 countries and written over 100 books with sales of more than 3 million copies. Toler for many years served as vice president and instructor for John C. Maxwell's INJOY Leadership Institute, training leaders how to make a difference in the world.